LECTURES ON DOSTOEVSKY

Lectures on
Dostoevsky

~

Joseph Frank

Edited by
Marina Brodskaya
and Marguerite Frank

PRINCETON UNIVERSITY PRESS
PRINCETON & OXFORD

Published by Princeton University Press
41 William Street, Princeton, New Jersey 08540
6 Oxford Street, Woodstock, Oxfordshire OX20 1TR

press.princeton.edu

Library of Congress Cataloging-in-Publication Data
Names: Brodskaya, Marina, 1957- author. | Frank, Marguerite, editor. |
    Frank, Joseph, 1918-2013, author.
Title: Lectures on Dostoevsky / Marina Brodskaya, Marguerite Frank,
    Joseph Frank.
Description: Princeton : Princeton University Press, 2019.
Identifiers: LCCN 2019020469 | ISBN 9780691178967 (hardcover)
Subjects: LCSH: Dostoyevsky, Fyodor, 1821-1881--Criticism and
    interpretation.
Classification: LCC PG3328.Z6 B685 2019 | DDC 891.73/3--dc23
LC record available at https://lccn.loc.gov/2019020469
ISBN (e-book): 9780691189567

British Library Cataloging-in-Publication Data is available

Editorial: Anne Savarese and Jenny Tan
Production Editorial: Ellen Foos
Text and Jacket Design: Leslie Flis
Production: Erin Suydam
Publicity: Jodi Price and Katie Lewis
Copyeditor: Aimee Anderson

Jacket art: Manuscript page from Dostoevsky's *Demons* (1871–1872)

This book has been composed in Arno Pro

Printed on acid-free paper. ∞

Printed in the United States of America

10 9 8 7 6 5 4 3 2 1

Grateful acknowledgment is made for permission to reprint "Joseph
Frank's Dostoevsky" from *Consider the Lobster and Other Essays* by David
Foster Wallace. Copyright © 2005 by David Foster Wallace. Used by
permission of Little, Brown and Company.

Figures 1 through 4 courtesy of the family of Joseph Frank.

CONTENTS

FOREWORD

In 2002, when Joseph Frank completed his five-volume literary biography of Dostoevsky, he joined the ranks of such biographers as Leon Edel (*Henry James: A Life*), Richard Ellmann (*James Joyce*), Walter Jackson Bate, (*John Keats*), Janet Browne (*Charles Darwin: A Biography*), not to mention James Boswell and his *Life of Johnson*. In any project spanning decades, one's view of one's subject changes, as does the cultural and critical climate surrounding the biographer himself. Frank's opus reflects both his evolving take on Dostoevsky—the writer, the thinker, the man—and his own development as a major critic of our time, one whose early preoccupations with theory gave way to his subsequent interest in creating, by the time he reached volume 5 (*Dostoevsky: The Mantle of the Prophet, 1871–1881*), an almost day-by-day account of the last decade of Dostoevsky's life. Readers can even indulge in drawing parallels between the number of pages of Frank's biography and those of Dostoevsky's novels or between the span of decades of each as well: there is a similarity of scale, a similarity of preoccupation with certain big themes and ideas, as well as movement forward in surprising new directions. Monumental biographies, such as Frank's Dostoevsky volumes, shape the way we understand not only a writer and his work but the world—both the subject's world and our own. Frank later worked to condense his hefty opus into a single-volume version that appeared in 2009: *Dostoevsky: A Writer in His Time* represents a fascinating distillation of literary analysis and cultural history.

But now, posthumously, a completely new distillation, in yet another genre—the lecture—has appeared. *Lectures on Dostoevsky* by Joseph Frank, edited by Marina Brodskaya and Marguerite Frank, renders an exquisite yet provocative series of Frank's lectures to his students at Stanford, where, astonishingly, only after his retirement from Princeton did he, arguably the world's most renowned Dostoevsky scholar, begin regularly to teach a course on Dostoevsky from within a Slavic department. (Years earlier, when visiting Harvard, he had offered a course on Dostoevsky.) The *Lectures* are a gift to general readers as well as to scholars of Dostoevsky, who will surely find themselves pondering the contrast between Frank's emphases in his critical writings and those in evidence in his lectures to students and a more broadly based reading public.

Joseph Frank was born in 1918 on the Lower East Side of Manhattan, an immigrant neighborhood where many of America's future intellectuals spent their childhoods. His father died when he was a young child, and he was adopted by his mother's second husband, William Frank. Those who knew Frank will remember that he suffered from an occasional stammer, which remarkably did not hamper his brilliance as a lecturer. Turning inward as a child, he became a voracious reader and, while still in high school, attended lectures at the New School for Social Research. His parents died when he was still a young man, and nearly penniless, he traveled to the University of Wisconsin where he had heard that the dean was sympathetic to Jewish students seeking an education. Amazingly, although he had never received a BA, he was accepted and earned a PhD at the University of Chicago from the famous Committee on Social Thought.

During the 1940s and beyond Frank began to publish a series of ground-breaking essays and quickly became recognized as one of the country's most promising literary critics and theorists. His essay "Spatial Form in Modern Literature," first published in 1945, remains a classic and formed the core of his seminal book, *The Widening Gyre: Crisis and Mastery in Modern Literature.* (This work appeared in a second edition with important additions and commentaries as *The Idea of Spatial Form* [1991]).

Frank wrote essays for the leading intellectual and literary journals in the United States (such as the *Sewanee Review*, the *Hudson Review*, the *Partisan Review*, and the *New Republic*) on an impressive range of artists and authors—Gide, Flaubert, Malraux, Mann, Goya, Cezanne, Sartre, Proust and, increasingly, Dostoevsky.

Many readers first encountered Frank's work on Dostoevsky through his unforgettable essays on *Notes from Underground*, *The Idiot*, and *The Possessed*. Reading these essays could change the way one read not only Dostoevsky but novels in general; both the work and oneself as general reader were simultaneously transformed. It turned out that reading Dostoevsky had already proved transformative for Frank as well: to the surprise and disappointment of some, Frank put aside his role as major theoretician and literary critic to write a literary biography of Dostoevsky—a biography whose creation spanned the next decades of his life, until 2002. He spent much of his final decade working on the single-volume condensation of the biography and writing essays that appeared in publications such as the *New York Review of Books*. He published three important collections of his essays, *Through the Russian Prism: Essays on Literature and Culture* (1989), *Between Religion and Rationality: Essays in Russian Literature and Culture* (2010), and *Responses to Modernity: Essays in the Politics of Culture* (2012).

Frank's work exhibits a thoughtful integrity, a willingness to follow the evidence wherever it led, even if that meant revising and rethinking a former position. He was a meticulous and creative close reader of texts who brought those readings to bear on the largest, most complex and pressing cultural, political, and social issues of Dostoevsky's time and, indirectly, of our own. Although his work on Dostoevsky is routinely hailed as "monumental," it should also be hailed as "finely observed and closely argued."

Frank thus came to Dostoevsky as a critic and theorist par excellence but also through a vital encounter with *Notes from Underground*. "My own attempt . . . began with *Notes from Underground*," he wrote. "It was in grappling with this text that I began to understand the complexity of the relations in [Dostoevsky's] writings between psychology and ideology, and how important it was for a proper comprehension of the first to identify its roots in the social-cultural context of the second" (*Dostoevsky: Mantle*, xii). Frank's fascination with the *Notes* is one of the primary intellectual underpinnings of his five-volume biography, and his sustained encounter with it seems as fundamental to his overall vision as does Dostoevsky's with the Book of Job. It sets the stage for his subsequent preoccupation with understanding the relations between psychology and ideology in Dostoevsky's work within the social-cultural context of his time. He discovers emanations of the Underground Man throughout Dostoevsky's future novels and journalism, especially *The Diary of a Writer*, not only in "A Gentle Creature" and "The Dream of a Ridiculous Man" but in the musings of "A Certain Person," as well as other works that do not figure in his *Lectures*.

In volume 3, *Dostoevsky: The Stir of Liberation, 1860–1865*, Frank makes a broad and categorical statement that, despite its ringing absolutes—its un-modern lack of qualifiers—has held true. Let me quote him:

Few works in modern literature are more widely read than Dostoevsky's *Notes from Underground* or so often cited as a key text revelatory of the hidden depth of the sensibility of our time. The term "underground man" has now become part of the vocabulary of contemporary culture, and this character has now achieved—like Hamlet, Don Quixote, Don Juan, and Faust—the stature of one of the great archetypal literary creations. . . . No book or essay dealing with the precarious situation of modern man would be complete without some allusion to Dostoevsky's explosive figure. Most important cultural developments of the present century—Nietzscheanism, Freudianism, Expressionism, Surrealism, Crisis Theology, Existentialism—have claimed the underground man as their own or have been linked with him by zealous interpreters; and when the underground man has not been hailed as a prophetic anticipation, he has been held up to exhibition as a luridly repulsive warning. The underground man has thus entered into the very warp and woof of modern culture in a fashion testifying to the philosophical suggestiveness and hypnotic power of this first great creation of Dostoevsky's post-Siberian years. At the same time, however, this widespread notoriety has given rise to a good deal of misunderstanding (3: 310).

Generations of readers have been captivated by Frank's bold argument that the Underground Man does not attempt to refute the ideas of the radicals of the 1860s so much as he is himself a representation of those ideas. This insight offers a compelling path into the labyrinth of Dostoevsky's creative mind.

How, then, does Frank choose to present *Notes from Underground,* a pivotal work for both Dostoevsky and for Frank, in the

Lectures? He distills a lifelong preoccupation with this complex novella into two lectures (chapter 4), the first of which devotes significant time to a lesser-known, nonfictional work, *Winter Notes on Summer Impressions*, in the context of part one, while the second lecture continues his engagement with part one of the novella, devoting only a few pages to its lengthier, more plot-driven part two. Yet the overall effect of the two lectures is one of balance and measure; what seems to be an idiosyncratic strategy ends by offering an unusually coherent and complete reading of the *Notes*. I leave it to the readers of these *Lectures* to discover Frank's strategy.

Nevertheless, I offer a few observations to accompany the reader of these two lectures. At the outset Frank barely lets on how important this "little masterpiece" will prove to be; he emphasizes instead how it "was hardly noticed when it was published" (chapter 4). Almost in passing he renders an important, highly original observation—that in Dostoevsky's previous work the reactions of the characters were determined by their place in the social hierarchy, but with the Underground Man specific ideological contexts become primary, setting the pattern for the later novels. Frank goes on to explain what to many has been Dostoevsky's mysterious, even incomprehensible, political shift away from the radical intelligentsia after his Siberian sojourn toward support of the tsar in stark, simple, but accurate terms: most important, according to Frank, was the tsar's abolition of serfdom, "the very aim of the revolutionary group to which Dostoevsky had belonged. Thus the tsar had accomplished Dostoevsky's own deepest wish, and from that time on, Dostoevsky became a loyal supporter of the tsarist regime" (chapter 4). Who but Frank is entitled to make such a simple, even reductive, explanation of a complex process—for he had already devoted several volumes of his massive biography toward understanding the subtleties and mysteries of the workings of Dostoevsky's political mind during precisely this period. It is in this lecture, moreover, that Frank introduces his notion of how the reader becomes a character in Dostoevsky's works, demonstrating the ways in which the narrator is ironic both about himself and his reader. He goes on to link the source of this "double irony" to what he labels "the *schizophrenia* of the educated Russians in relation to European culture, which they both admire and resent" (chapter 4).

Only in his second lecture on the *Notes* does Frank reveal that it has been his own past analysis of this work that has shifted the general understanding of it, and that revelation occurs in parentheses. (Perhaps he never even bothered to read that aside to his students.) A hallmark of these lectures throughout is their modesty, coupled with his unceasing effort to express complex ideas—ideas about Dostoevsky and his time, about which Frank has remained the authority for several decades—simply and clearly so that any student or general reader can understand them. Yet these *Lectures* represent no dumbing down of the subject; they abound with surprising observations that suggest future directions other Dostoevsky readers might choose to follow.

Each of these lectures has its pithy insights, offered up almost in passing. Frank understands the action of *Crime and Punishment*, for example, as "constructed so as to reveal Raskolnikov to himself, to allow him to solve the mystery contained in his own character. The book really depicts the coming-to-consciousness of . . . Raskolnikov, about the truth of his own behavior, the *real* meaning of what he has done compared to the *initial* meaning that he thought his actions would have" (chapter 5). With *The Idiot*, however, Frank finds that "what makes the book so remarkable is that the ideal and absolute value that Dostoevsky is testing here happens to be *his* own" (chapter 6)—an insight tossed in practically as an aside. Frank unhesitatingly places Dostoevsky's final novel, *The Brothers Karamazov*, among the most enduring creations of the Western literary tradition: the *Divine Comedy, Paradise Lost, King Lear, Faust.* "These are the comparisons that spring to mind," he tells his students. From a series of lectures that grounded Dostoevsky's works in the intricacies of Russian history and culture, Frank now expands his analysis to a broader canvas, while continuing to explore the novel through the prism of the Russian experience. It is a complex juggling feat, and one that Frank seems to perform almost without effort, the way a poet—for example, Yeats in "The Circus Animal's Desertion"—can synthesize the specific and the universal into one seamless whole.

Readers may by this point begin to wonder how Frank will find a way to end these spectacular lectures. He does so by borrowing (or, as Dostoevsky would have it in *The Brothers Karamazov*, by committing an act of benign and fruitful plagiarism: Jesus kisses the Grand Inquisitor; Alyosha kisses Ivan). Frank, too, seals his narrative with the kiss of forgiveness, now transferred from characters to author: "This kiss, in my view, represents Dostoevsky's own attitude to the new radicals, whom he was prepared to forgive but not to accept" (chapter 7).

Frank had always been generically bold: he turned from theory to biography—from a hot new form to a more old-fashioned one. He made the genre of biography new again, helping to ignite our general fascination with cultural history. And now we have his *Lectures.* Few professors these days boast of giving lectures: they are just another outmoded form. Now the task is to encourage student participation, even in the largest of courses. But Frank created his *Lectures on Dostoevsky* and in so doing breathed new life into an old form.

How different these lectures are from Nabokov's idiosyncratic *Lectures on Russian Literature*, with which they will inevitably be compared. These two volumes, both published posthumously, do not occupy the same critical universe, although they each privilege the work over the author, albeit in vastly contrasting ways. In the preface to the first volume of his Dostoevsky biography, Frank wrote, "My work is not a biography, or if so, only in a special sense—for I do not go from the life to the work, but rather the other way round. My purpose is to interpret Dostoevsky's art, and this purpose commands my choice of detail and my perspective" (1: xii). Or, as Nabokov famously said, in writing about Dickens, "Let us be thankful for the web and ignore the spider" (*Lectures on Literature*, 65). Frank's penetrating scrutiny of that web eventually led him to an unparalleled understanding not only of the spider but also of its surrounding flora and fauna.

Yet Frank is never cute, never openly opinionated, never seeking to shock or pierce the heart. Unlike Nabokov, his Dostoevsky is not the creator "of wastelands of literary platitudes" whom he is "very eager to debunk" (*Lectures on Russian Literature*, 98) and whom he imagines sitting outside his door waiting to discuss his low grade. ("Tolstoy is the greatest Russian writer of prose fiction. Leaving aside his precursors Pushkin and Lermontov, we might list the greatest artists in Russian prose thus: first, Tolstoy; second, Gogol; third, Chekhov; fourth, Turgenev. This is rather like grading students' papers and no doubt Dostoevsky and Saltykov are waiting at the door of my office to discuss their low marks" (*Lectures on Russian Literature*, 137).) Frank never gains points at the expense of his subject. Nabokov's impish, frequently perverse, brilliant lectures reveal a being who inserts himself into the warp and woof, the intimate texture of the creative works at hand. Frank's lectures, while equally brilliant, aim always to render Dostoevsky's works accessible to his students so that each may individually find a path toward creating their own Dostoevsky. He wears his immense knowledge lightly; he renders the complex into the seemingly simple; he does not insert himself into the work but chooses instead to offer steady support to the student or the reader through imagining his subject not outside his office door but immersed in his own time and place while endeavoring to embody both the everyday and the eternal questions in his fiction. Frank's intellectual generosity quietly, unobtrusively shines forth, not to dazzle, like Nabokov, but to illuminate.

In conclusion we may return full circle to *Notes from Underground* and the invitation Frank received in 1955 to give a Gauss Seminar at Princeton, where he chose the *Notes* as his subject. Frank's *Lectures* have a kinship to those of Christian Gauss, whose teaching style, as Edmund Wilson observed, included an unusual "fluidity of mind" and an ability to encourage in his students "trains of thought" that led them to find their own conclusions (*Masters*, 3–4): "[E]xtreme flexibility and enormous range were . . . a feature of his lectures. . . . He would show you what the author was aiming at and the methods he had adopted to achieve his ends" (*Masters*, 6). Wilson quotes a former student who became a distinguished federal judge; he described his teacher's intellectual integrity: "He gave me the vision of language and literature as something representing the continuous and never-ending flow of man's struggle to think the thoughts which, when put into action, constitute in the aggregate the advance of civilization" (*Masters*, 17). Joseph Frank's intellectual rigor combines in these *Lectures* with a seeming ease and fluidity of pacing that is in fact carefully constructed. Without fireworks and brinksmanship, without trying overly hard to engage in classroom

theatrics, he offers up both himself and his subject as representations of the value of intellectual, philosophical, and aesthetic
inquiry.

Robin Feuer Miller
Brandeis University

Works Cited

Part of this foreword is adapted from my essays "Frank's Dostoevsky" (*Slavic and East European Journal* 47, no. 3 (2003): 471–
79) and "Joseph Frank" (*Dostoevsky Studies*, New Series, 18
(2014): 9–22).

Joseph Frank, *Dostoevsky: A Writer in His Time* (Princeton: Princeton University Press,
2009).
——*Dostoevsky: The Mantle of the Prophet* (Princeton: Princeton University Press,
2002).
——*Dostoevsky: The Stir of Liberation: 1860–1865* (Princeton: Princeton University
Press, 1986).
——*Dostoevsky: The Seeds of Revolt 1821–1849* (Princeton: Princeton University
Press, 1976).
Vladimir Nabokov, *Lectures on Literature*, edited by Fredson Bowers, introduction by
John Updike (New York: Harcourt, 1980).
——*Lectures on Russian Literature*, edited and with an introduction by Fredson
Bowers (New York: Harcourt, 1981).
Edmund Wilson, "Christian Gauss," in *Masters: Portraits of Great Teachers*, edited by
Joseph Epstein (New York: Basic Books, 1981).

PREFACE

Professor Joseph Frank was teaching his annual ten-week seminar called "Dostoevsky and His Times," at Stanford University and I was teaching a graduate-level Russian language course using *Crime and Punishment*. At the end of my class, I would head straight for Joseph Frank's seminar room on the Main Quad, taking a seat around a large oval table along with his students.

He didn't ask questions; he didn't solicit opinions. He would sit down, often sporting a *Crime & Punishment* baseball cap, which he would then remove and place on the table next to his notes. He would look around the room and then start speaking—"In the last lecture . . ."—beautifully weaving the prior week's material to the lecture he was about to give. He spoke slowly, stammering occasionally. The notes in front of him were his lectures: carefully crafted, handwritten or typed, but always purposeful, controlled, illuminating, and wide ranging. Joseph Frank's Dostoevsky emerged as both a radical and a conservative, a prisoner and a prophet, who, like each one of us sitting around the oval table, was a product of their contemporaneous world. I suggested that we put his Dostoevsky course in the form of a book, an idea that Joseph Frank readily embraced. We knew it would be an unusual book.

But then Joseph Frank's career was also unusual in many ways. His first literary articles appeared in 1938 in the *Washington Square Review*, a student publication at New York University,

FIGURE 1. The lectures in this book come from a seminar Joseph Frank taught at Stanford University called "Dostoevsky and His Times."

FIGURE 2. Frank worked as a journalist before
pursuing a PhD.

where he was listed an editor—although he was never a regis-
tered student. Between 1942 and 1950 he worked as a journalist
in Washington, DC, covering social, economic, and legal issues
for the Bureau of National Affairs. At the same time, he continued to pursue his scholarly interests on the side, culminating
with the publication in the *Sewanee Review* of "Spatial Form in
Modern Literature: An Essay in Three Parts," which quickly
became a landmark in the study of modern literature.

FIGURE 3. Frank wrote his five-volume
biography of Dostoevsky while teaching
comparative literature at Princeton University.

Along with sudden critical fame, he was awarded in 1950 a
Fulbright fellowship to France. It was there that he met his future
wife, Marguerite, a Harvard Ph.D. candidate in mathematics, who
(together with her co-author Philip Wolfe) published the
Frank-Wolfe algorithm for quadratic programming, a method
used in high-speed machine computations.[1]

Upon returning to the United States, Joseph Frank continued to contribute articles on contemporary writers to *Partisan
Review* and the *New Republic*, among others journals, obtained
his Ph.D., and began teaching. A turning point for him came

1. Frank, M.; Wolfe, P. (1956). "An algorithm for quadratic programming". *Naval
Research Logistics Quarterly*. 3 (1–2): 95–110. doi:10.1002/nav.3800030109.

when Princeton University invited him to give a Gauss Seminar in Criticism, and he chose to discuss *Notes from Underground*. Rejecting the existential interpretation of the work prevalent at the time, he instead focused on the intellectual, ideological, and political world of Dostoevsky. A few years after giving the seminar, he was invited to join the Princeton faculty and direct the Gauss Seminars in Criticism.

A non-Slavist at Princeton, teaching courses in English and comparative literature, he succeeded in acquiring a reading knowledge of Russian (a Russian-English dictionary and a grammar book always by his side, even at the beach) in order to expand his research on Dostoevsky. This research ultimately turned into a five-volume literary biography of the writer, published by Princeton University Press over a period of 25 years. Among all the praise his multi-volume work received, it was an unconventional article in an unexpected publication, the *Village Voice*, that delighted him most. The essay, "Joseph Frank's Dostoevsky" was written by David Foster Wallace and it is included at the end of this volume.

Upon retirement from Princeton, Joseph Frank was invited to Stanford University to give an annual course on Dostoevsky, and the lectures in this book represent the content of that course. After Joseph Frank died, I asked Marguerite Frank to work with me on the lectures. We deciphered and edited his handwritten notes, provided translation, references, and additional necessary material. Inspired by his keen interest in screen adaptations of Dostoevsky's work, we also included a list of selected films to complement the readings.

Joseph Frank's approach to Dostoevsky has never been more relevant, as moral and political instability and latent nihilism become more prevalent with each generation. The lectures

FIGURE 4. Joseph Frank at Fyodor Dostoevsky's grave,
Tikhvin Cemetery, St. Petersburg, Russia.

convey his insights, his enthusiasm for teaching, and his contri-
bution to a deeper understanding of the great writer. Whether
you are an independent reader, a teacher, or a student of literature, these lectures are for you.

Marina Brodskaya
Stanford, 2019

Introductory Lecture

The aim of this course is to read several of Dostoevsky's best-known works and in this way to introduce the main literary and ideological elements of his work.

Dostoevsky is not a writer to struggle through or with, but one who tries to make his work as interesting and exciting—and as readable—as possible. His works raise some of the deepest moral and philosophical issues of Western culture, but he also wanted to keep his readers interested.

For one thing, it was necessary for him to do so. He was the only important Russian writer of his time who wrote for a living, and his income was dependent on his popularity. As a result, he used devices like mystery and suspense, techniques ordinarily associated with types of narrative written for a mass audience, for serious themes that rivaled what can be found in poetic tragedy. Actually, in doing so he was following in the footsteps of non-Russians like Hugo, Balzac, and Dickens, who also dealt with serious moral and social issues and used such mystery-story or adventure-story techniques.

The gap between the two kinds of literature was much wider in Russia than in Europe, probably because there was no real mass audience in Russia—most of the population was illiterate—and books circulated largely only among the upper classes. This situation changed, of course, as time went on. But this is one reason Dostoevsky remains one of the most widely read of the Russian classic writers throughout the world, and the list of screen and stage adaptations based on his works grows every year. Among the great writers of the nineteenth century, Dostoevsky seems the most contemporary to present-day readers. It is as if his works do not deal with issues of the past but are directly relevant to those of the present day.

We certainly don't have this feeling of contemporaneity when reading someone like Tolstoy. We can easily identify with what may be called the universal problems of civilized life as they appear in Tolstoy's novels, but the world in which Tolstoy's main characters live is totally different from Dostoevsky's. It is the world of the Russian past.

The world of Dostoevsky, on the other hand, is a world in constant flux and change, in which the stability of the past, anchored by a belief in God, has begun to be seriously questioned. It is a world in which new ideas and ideologies have begun to influence the minds and hearts of a new group called the *intelligentsia*, that is, educated people who no longer felt a part of the old socioreligious structures and wanted to change them in fundamental ways. Dostoevsky attacked this group in his major novels, but he understood them from the inside at the same time. One of our aims will be to understand how he could both oppose them but also depict them with so much sympathy, inner comprehension, and even pity.

The world of Dostoevsky is thus inwardly much closer to our own, which may be said to have begun after the end of the First World War in 1918. It was then that the self-confidence of Western European civilization collapsed, and the problems raised in Dostoevsky's novels, which earlier had seemed to be only peculiarly *Russian*, became those of our Western culture as a whole.

Another aim is to study Dostoevsky's works in relation to their literary and ideological contexts, so as to bring out what he was trying to express or convey in relation to his own times. Like all great writers, his works go far beyond their historical context, and

I shall try to give you a sense of these larger issues as well, as they appeared to him in his own period.

Russian Culture

Early Russian literature was mostly theological, controlled by religious and Christian ideas and values derived from Byzantine Christianity. It remained under this influence to a great extent until the arrival of Peter the Great in the late seventeenth century. Peter the Great insisted that the literate class, roughly the nobility who governed the country, reeducate itself according to the Western and European norms of the time. This led to all kinds of changes in customs, but what is most important for us is that it meant adopting the ideas of rationalism that had begun to predominate in European thought.

In Europe, the conflict between science and religion had reached some sort of compromise over the previous several centuries, but the change occurred much more quickly and despotically in Russia. For one thing, it only affected the small, literate ruling class, not the vast majority of the people, who were illiterate peasants. This created a split in Russian culture between the ruling class and the people, who lived in different moral and spiritual worlds. Everyone was aware of this split, but Dostoevsky experienced it deeply and personally in a unique way. When he was arrested in 1849 and sent to a prison camp to live with peasant convicts, he became aware of how wide this gap was. He and the few other educated prisoners were completely alienated from the peasant-convicts and were regarded almost as foreigners. They were also looked on with a hatred that could never have been openly expressed in ordinary social life. After this, Dostoevsky felt that the most important issue in Russian life was to bridge this gap; and to do so the educated class would have to come to respect the religious beliefs and values of the peasantry. He was not alone in this, and we can find the same theme emerging in Tolstoy.

During the nineteenth century, as a result of their European education, the ruling class began to have contempt for their own culture and the Russian language. It was the sign of a good education to speak French rather than Russian. One can see this in the beginning of Tolstoy's *War and Peace*, in which the aristocratic characters talk in French about the Napoleonic invasion. This level of Westernization within the ruling class itself led to an opposition between the so-called *Westernizers* and the *Slavophils*.

The first believed that Russia should follow the same social and political course as Europe. The second group thought that Russia had its own national particularities that should be developed and cultivated and not given up for the European model. As for Dostoevsky, we can say roughly that he began as a Westernizer but developed into a Slavophil. But although he sympathized with many Slavophil ideas, he never accepted all their doctrines.

An important reason is that the Slavophils tended to glorify and idealize the Russian past, which included serfdom.[1] He always retained some of the Westernizer aims of his early years, but he believed they could be realized without any political changes such as the weakening of tsarism. He did not think that any kind of constitutional democracy in the Western sense, or any other

1. Russian serfdom has its origins in the eleventh century, but landowners gained almost unlimited ownership over Russian serfs in the seventeenth and eighteenth centuries. Serfs were given to estates, and fleeing the estate was a criminal offense. Landowners were allowed to transfer and sell their serfs to other landowners, separating family members and keeping the serfs' property for themselves. Serfdom was abolished in 1861 under Tsar Alexander II.

kind of democratic system, was suitable for Russia, but he was always in favor of more freedom of speech and press. What he wanted most of all, once serfdom had been abolished in 1861, was that more land should be distributed to the peasantry. This was the cause of most of the social unrest, and Dostoevsky continued to believe until his death that the tsarist government would ultimately take the necessary steps to avoid disaster.

Biography

Before a discussion of Dostoevsky's first important book, *Poor Folk,* a few words must be said about his early life. My approach will be primarily cultural and ideological, but some events of his life are indeed of crucial importance.

He was born in 1821, to a family that had acquired the education necessary for status in Russian society. His father was an army doctor, and his mother came from a well-educated merchant family. Dostoevsky's father attained the status of a nobleman, but this was a civil service ranking in Russia, which did not give him the status of landowning families, in which the rank of nobility was inherited. This may help to explain why Dostoevsky was so sensitive to the theme of social humiliation, especially in his early works.

Another important aspect of these early years is his religious education. Dostoevsky's father came from a family of Russian Orthodox priests and was very devout. His mother was also religious, and Dostoevsky himself later referred to this background as important for him. A tutor came to the house to teach him and his brother French, but so did a priest, to instruct them in the Orthodox faith. This was quite different from the usual pattern of the inherited nobility, whose Western education, primarily French, had made them more or less indifferent to religion. Late in his life Dostoevsky wrote of the importance of the religious education he had received from his parents and of the religious pilgrimages on which he was taken by his mother. Dostoevsky and his brother were sent to very good private schools, and the parents also read to them every night from both the Russian classics and European works translated into Russian.

His father decided that Dostoevsky should become a military engineer, and he was sent to study in St. Petersburg for such a career. But he had already made up his mind that he wanted to become a writer, and while he passed his courses in technical subjects, he was more interested in the literary ones that were also given in the school.

An important event in 1839 was the death of his father, who was rumored to have been murdered by the peasant serfs on their small estate in the country. Officially, it was specified that he died of an apoplectic fit. A good deal has been made of this rumored murder, and it was very important for Freud, who wrote a famous article, "Dostoevsky and Parricide," analyzing its presumed importance on Dostoevsky's character and his work, especially *The Brothers Karamazov*.

Dostoevsky graduated from the academy and served as an army engineer, but he was apparently not very good at the job. He resigned his commission when he inherited a small amount of money. His first novel was a success and made him famous overnight. After that he lived on advances and payment for his work; he called himself "a literary proletarian."[2]

2. In a letter to N. N. Strakhov dated September 30, 1863, from Rome, Dostoevsky wrote, "I am a literary proletarian, and whoever wants my work must provide payment upfront."

The success of his first novel brought Dostoevsky into contact with the important critic Vissarion Belinsky[3] and introduced
him to a group of young writers influenced by radical and socialist ideas. Two years later he quarreled with Belinsky both for
literary reasons and because of atheism. Dostoevsky refused
Belinsky's acceptance of a totally atheistic position under the
influence of the German philosopher Ludwig Feuerbach, who
had declared that, instead of God having created humanity, it
was humanity that had created the idea of God.[4]

Dostoevsky then began to attend meetings of the Petrashevsky Circle, a gathering of young men who met once a week
to discuss advanced European ideas. Most of them were disci-
ples of the French socialist Charles Fourier, who did not believe
in revolutionary violence but wanted to create a brave new world
by example.[5] Dostoevsky did not accept any of these socialist
programs because he thought they interfered with the freedom
of the individual personality. But he stood out within the group
by his violent hatred of serfdom.

That hatred helps to explain why he joined with eight others
to form a secret society within this group, whose aim was to stir
up a revolution against serfdom. But the plans of the secret
society were stopped when all of the Petrashevsky Circle
were arrested following the revolutions in Europe in 1848.
The existence of the revolutionary secret society was not discovered at the time and only came to light in 1922, long after

3. Vissarion Belinsky (1811–1848), a Russian literary critic and editor.

4. Ludwig Feuerbach (1804–1872), a German philosopher and the author of *The
Essence of Christianity* (1842).

5. The Petrashevsky Circle was named for its organizer, Mikhail Petrashevsky
(1821–1866), a follower of François Marie Charles Fourier (1772–1837), a French utopian socialist philosopher.

Dostoevsky's death. But Dostoevsky lived all his life with the knowledge that he, too, had once consented to unleashing murder through a revolution, and his deep understanding of the psychology of such characters in his novels can surely be attributed to this cause.

Dostoevsky spent about a year in solitary confinement after his arrest. As a nobleman he was well treated but then taken out to face a firing squad, only to have his life spared in the last minute.[6] He was then sentenced to a four-year prison term at hard labor, after which he served in the Russian army as a soldier and then became an officer again. His years in the prison camp, following the mock execution, were of decisive importance in reshaping his spiritual and ideological views. These years also were the inspiration for one of his least-read but most important works, a sort of novelistic autobiography, *House of the Dead*, which Tolstoy later called one of the greatest masterpieces of Russian literature.

Literary Background

Dostoevsky became a writer at a particular period of Russian literature, and it's important to locate him in this context if we wish to understand his work. Speaking very broadly, we can say that, along with the change in Russian culture as a whole initiated by the reforms of Peter the Great, Russian literature more or less followed suit, adapting European literary styles to Rus-

6. Dostoevsky was imprisoned in Peter and Paul Fortress in St. Petersburg, established by Peter the Great in 1703. From around 1720, the fort served as a prison for high-ranking or political prisoners.

sian material. During Dostoevsky's boyhood, the great writer A. S. Pushkin took Byron and Shakespeare as his models and showed how original masterpieces could be created out of the transformation of these models to express typically Russian themes.[7]

Popular novels also were written in this high Romantic style, and there are parodistic references to this in *Poor Folk*. But in the early 1840s, the critic Belinsky began to argue that Russian writers should follow the example of European writers like Balzac, George Sand, and Dickens. They focused on the social problems of their own times and society, and thus helped, as we say these days, to raise the consciousness of their readers about such problems.

Belinsky made this point most forcefully in writing about Nikolay Gogol, whose novel *Dead Souls* and whose short story *The Overcoat* he held up as an example for Russian writers to follow.[8] Dostoevsky was already an admirer of Balzac; his first published work was a translation of that French novelist's *Eugenie Grandet* (1833). He was also a great admirer of Gogol, and the main character of *Poor Folk* is of the same social type as that of Gogol's *The Overcoat*. But in the case of Dostoevsky, one can say that he not only wore the overcoat but turned it inside out.

7. Alexander Sergeyevich Pushkin (1799–1837), a poet, playwright, and novelist widely considered to be the founder of modern literature in Russia.

8. Nikolay Vasilyevich Gogol (1809–1852), one of the preeminent figures of Russian literary realism. His later writing openly satirizes political and spiritual corruption in the Russian Empire, which eventually prompted him to leave Russia and live in Italy from 1836 to 1848.

Other Literary Influences

Two other writers important for understanding the first work we are going to discuss are Nikolay Karamzin and Pushkin.[9] Both are related to *Poor Folk*, and this fact tells us something important about Dostoevsky, namely that he is a writer who creates out of his own personal experience and who recasts such experience in terms furnished by the culture and ideas of his time. He invariably provides cultural clues, as it were, to help us to understand the meaning of his works. He wishes us to grasp them not only in terms of the individual psychology or conflicts of his characters but also in relation to the wider meaning they convey in the Russian cultural environment.

Karamzin is little known outside Russia, but he was an important writer who exercised a wide influence. He wrote not only stories but an important travel book, *Letters of a Russian Traveler*, and a history of Russia in an accessible modern style that celebrated tsarism as the only reasonable kind of government for a country as large as Russia. Dostoevsky said late in life that he had grown up on Karamzin, and the same is true for most of the generation of the 1840s. Karamzin is linked to *Poor Folk* because one of his most famous stories is called *Poor Liza*, and it also deals compassionately with the fate of the humble and oppressed lower class in Russia.

In *Poor Liza*, a highly idealized peasant girl who sells flowers in the streets, the epitome of all the graces and virtues, falls in love with a young aristocrat who courts her but then makes a wealthy marriage to a member of his own class. Poor Liza then drowns herself in the lake of a monastery garden in which they

9. Nikolay Karamzin (1765–1826), a Russian writer, poet, historian, and critic, best known for his twelve-volume *History of the Russian State*.

used to meet. Apparently this garden then became a favorite place for romantic meetings and family picnics because of the popularity of the story. Dostoevsky's title reminded his readers of this story. His style and treatment are totally different, and the details are much harsher and cruder, but Dostoevsky's story essentially makes the same point in its own way.

Another writer mentioned in *Poor Folk* is Pushkin. The young Dostoevsky adored him, and when Pushkin was killed in a duel, in the same year as Dostoevsky's mother's death, Dostoevsky said he would have worn mourning for Pushkin if he were not already doing so for his mother. In the very last year of Dostoevsky's life, he made a famous speech declaring that Pushkin was as great a writer as Shakespeare, Cervantes, or Goethe, and in some ways even greater.[10]

Pushkin's short story "The Stationmaster" is one of the inspirations for *Poor Folk*. The initial story again shows the influence of sentimentalism and can be seen as a continuation of the theme of *Poor Liza,* that is, the helplessness of the lower classes in the face of the power and authority of those above them. It has the same aim of eliciting sympathy for what Dostoevsky later called *the insulted and injured.* Here once again a lower-class girl, the daughter of a stationmaster whose job is to look after the changing of horses in the carriages of travelers, is seduced by a passing nobleman. In this case, he takes her away from her father, sets her up as his mistress, and treats her very well. But the old father is heartbroken by what he considers to be the debasement of his daughter. Repulsed when he tries to persuade her to return, he takes to drink and dies of grief. Later, she comes back to weep on his grave. Again, attention is directed to the sad plight of the

10. Dostoyevsky delivered the Pushkin Speech in 1880 at the unveiling of the Pushkin monument in Moscow.

lower classes, their equal capacity with their social superiors for deep feeling, and their helplessness.

Another writer referred to explicitly in *Poor Folk* is Gogol, and the background here requires a little more detail. The mid-1840s began what has been called the Gogol period of Russian literature. Dostoevsky was following very closely the new literary trends.

One of the types of writing that the literary critic Belinsky praised was "physiological sketches." These are descriptions of ordinary city life and of the lives of very ordinary people who carry out the daily tasks that make existence possible for their superiors—such as a house porter sweeping away the snow or an organ grinder walking through the streets and playing his music. No one had thought such insignificant people worthy of literary attention in the past. Or if they appeared, they were inevitably comic types at whom the reader was supposed to laugh.

The critic Belinsky had urged younger Russian writers to follow Gogol's example, whose main character in "The Overcoat," the clerk Akakii, is someone existing on the very lowest rung of the Russian social ladder. He is a member of the army of clerks who worked for the Russian bureaucracy in Petersburg and kept the empire going. The narrator who tells his story is quite superior and ironic about him and makes the reader feel the same way. The copyist is perfectly happy in his job and even continues to copy at home because he enjoys it so much. But when he is asked to summarize the ideas in one of the documents he is copying, he finds it too difficult to do.

Gogol is writing about the lower classes, but he hardly portrays his character in any sort of favorable light. Other young clerks in the bureau make fun of him, tease and torment him, and from time to time he protests and asks: "What have I done to you?" A new young clerk is so moved by this complaint that "in these penetrating words he heard the echo of other words: "I am your brother." This note of Christian compassion is introduced very briefly and on the side, as it were, but we are told that it left a permanent impression on the younger man.

What happens is that Akakii needs to have a new overcoat made because his old one is so worn out that it doesn't protect him against the Russian winter. This new coat costs so much that he has to cut down on meals to save for it, and when it's finally made he is so proud of it that it changes his life. His officemates begin to treat him with a little more respect because he no longer looks so ragged, and he is on the point of becoming human when the coat is stolen one night. He complains to the local commissioner of police, but nobody pays any attention to him. He is finally thrown out, falls ill, and soon dies. But there is a kind of semisupernatural ending, quite typical for Gogol, because from that time on the district where Akakii lost his coat is haunted by presumed phantoms who steal the coats of everybody passing that way. This only ends when the coat of the commissioner of police who had thrown Akakii out of his office is stolen, though phantoms now continue to appear in other districts. Just who and what they are is never very clear, but a reader of the time probably took all this as a satirical reference to the inefficiency and corruption of the police.

Dostoevsky follows in this tradition by writing about characters on the same social level, thus following Belinsky's advice. But he transforms these characters by combining the social pathos of Pushkin with the bureaucratic world of Gogol. Most important of all, he abandons the upper-class narrator who appears in both stories and adopts a form that allows the reader to enter into this lower-class world from the inside. We'll talk about that in the next lecture.

CHAPTER 1

Poor Folk

~

Dostoevsky's first novel was an important event in Russian literature. Later in life he reminisced about how *Poor Folk* came to the attention of the literary and social critic Vissarion Belinsky. Dostoevsky had lent the manuscript to two young writers (one of them, the poet Nikolay Nekrasov, soon became very famous himself), and the two were so impressed that they took the manuscript in the middle of the night to Belinsky, announcing to him that a new Gogol had been born. What they saw was a connection between this work and Belinsky's public view of how Russian literature should develop. But this does not mean that the connection between Dostoevsky and Gogol was that of follower to that of a literary leader. *Poor Folk* is as much a certain reaction against Gogol's satirical approach to his characters as it is a continuation of the literary example that Gogol set.

The novel is presented as an exchange of letters between two characters, Makar Devushkin and Varvara Dobroselova. The epistolary form was very popular in the eighteenth century, although somewhat out of date in 1845. Dostoevsky chose this particular form because it has some relevance to his thematic purpose. Dostoevsky was trying to endow his poor and humble characters with human dignity. Famous examples of the epistolary novel—such as Richardson's *Clarissa*, Rousseau's *La Nouvelle Héloïse*, and Choderlos de Laclos's *Les Liaisons Dangereuses*—depicted the lives of upper class and aristocratic characters, who had the leisure and the education to spend their time writing long letters to each other. By the choice of this form, Dostoevsky was implicitly saying that even a clerk on the very lowest level and a young girl who came from a very poor background (though she had been educated) have the same refined feelings and sensitivities as those originating from a much higher social level.

There is, however, another feature of the epistolary form that is also important to note. The writers of these letters express themselves not only eloquently but also without the explicit intervention of the author. The characters here convey their thoughts and feelings directly, unlike in a novel in which we have a third-person narrator. The reader is introduced immediately into their consciousness and into their images of themselves and their reactions to the world. This will be a particular feature of Dostoevsky's technique as a writer even when, as will be the case later, he does use a third-person narrator.

Except for a minor short story in the 1840s, Dostoevsky never used the epistolary technique again, though he does include letters as part of a larger text. It is important to note that even when he does have a third-person narrator, that role is reduced to a minimum. His characters usually express themselves as directly as they do in these letters, either through monologues (often speaking to themselves, as it were) or in dialogues with other characters. Dostoevsky is thus often called a "dramatic" writer because of this importance of direct dialogue in his work. A Russian literary critic, Mikhail Bakhtin, in his *Problems of Dostoevsky's Poetics*, has credited Dostoevsky with creating a new form of novel, a "polyphonic" novel, because of his preference for letting his characters express themselves directly, each in his or her own way. Bakhtin is an important and interesting figure whose ideas have exercised a considerable influence not only in Russia but around the world. Bakhtin does have penetrating

insights into particular features of Dostoevsky, but his general-
izations are unacceptable, and his claim that Dostoevsky inven-
ted an entirely new form of the novel always seemed to me
grossly exaggerated.[1]

Most importantly, *Poor Folk* created so much excitement
because it was the first really important work produced by a
writer of the Natural School. Typically, that kind of writing consisted of physiological sketches that had little, if any, story line
or were at most very brief short stories. Yet *Poor Folk* is not a
sketch but a novel, in which the lives of the two main characters
are depicted and a wide range of other characters allows the
reader to catch glimpses of the hardships endured by even the
educated lower rungs of the social order in the capital,
St. Petersburg.

The main male character, Makar Devushkin, is a middle-aged
file clerk whose last name in Russian means "a young, unmarried
woman, or a maiden," so it functions as both funny and ironic
at the same time. And the female character, Varvara Dobroselova, whose last name means "of a good, kind village, or spread-
ing goodness," is a young girl on her own and trying to earn a few
kopeks as a seamstress. Why she is in this position only becomes
clear later from the diary insert.

The two protagonists are very distant relations, and although
it becomes clear that he is in love with her, he is aware that the
age difference makes any closer and wished-for relations impossible. But in order to help her financially, he has fallen into
poverty himself, and in the first letters we see him trying to convince Varvara that he is not really sacrificing himself or suffering
on her behalf while, in fact, everything he says indicates the op-

---

1. Joseph Frank, *Through the Russian Prism: Essays on Literature and Culture*
(Princeton, NJ: Princeton University Press, 1989).

posite to be true. His inner struggle is revealed stylistically, as he keeps on contradicting himself all the time. And the more he denies something, the more it becomes clear through the details he provides that "the new warmer place" is actually a corner of a kitchen in an overcrowded rooming house and that he gave up his room and has been sinking lower and lower while struggling to preserve his self-respect. There is an inverse relation here with Gogol's *The Overcoat* that should be pointed out. Akakii Akakiyevich Bashmachkin's life is comically changed for the better momentarily because he acquires a new overcoat. Devushkin's life is transformed for the worse by his love and self-sacrifice for another human being. Also, there could not be a greater contrast with Gogol's hero, whose preoccupation with himself and lack of interest in the world around him attest to the limitations of his mind and character.

Both Devushkin and Varvara are so particularly sensitive to their surroundings that they at times do not see each other for fear of arousing suspicion that they might be carrying on an immoral affair. Despite their lowly social status, both are interested in what is being written and published contemporaneously, and this allows Dostoevsky to place them (and their story) in the context of the Russian literature of the time.

What had occurred with Varvara is conveyed only indirectly, but Dostoevsky expected his nineteenth-century readers to understand what he could not say explicitly for reasons of censorship. Varvara is seventeen and her past is revealed in her diary insert, which also contains the standard country-city contrast that goes back to the beginning of Western literature. The country is the place of childhood, therefore of innocence, and the city that of corruption and immorality.

Varvara comes with her parents to St. Petersburg, and after their death she is taken in by Anna Fyodorovna, a distant relative, who seems to live better than anyone might have expected, while the sources of her income and capital remain a mystery. People constantly come and go in that house, it seems, and earlier, Varvara's mother refused to have anything to do with its occupants. Dostoevsky thus indicates indirectly that this relative is engaged in shady affairs, such as the arrangement of sexual encounters between older men and innocent young girls like Varvara. And this is precisely what happened to Varvara: she was raped by a close friend of Anna Fyodorovna, the landowner Bykov (whose last name in Russian means "bull") and no longer wishes to stay there with Anna Fyodorovna.

There are other people who live in or visit the same house: Varvara's slightly younger cousin Sasha, also an orphan and someone who is destined for the same kind of fate as has befallen Varvara. Two other figures are quite important. One is Old Pokrovsky (the Russian word *pokrov* means "cover, protection, or intercession"), the first of many such characters in Dostoevsky's works, often referred to as "buffoons." Old Pokrovsky comes closest of all to resembling Gogol's Akakii Akakiyevich, but here again we see that though he is the lowest of the low, he looks troubled by his conscience. An inveterate drunkard, Old Pokrovsky is ashamed at his own debasement, which shows that he is not at all deprived of an awareness of finer feelings or has lost his sense of conscience. And this character type will be much developed all through Dostoevsky's later work.

Old Pokrovsky is supposed to be the father of young Pokrovsky, the tubercular student on whom Varvara obviously had a girlish crush and who dies at the end of Varvara's diary sequence. A careful reading shows, however, that the landowner Bykov had known the student's beautiful mother before her marriage to Pokrovsky, and Bykov somehow continued to look after the young man after her death. Once again, the reader fills in what

Dostoevsky as author could not say: Young Pokrovsky is Bykov's illegitimate son, and his mother was married off by Anna Fyodorovna to the penniless ex-clerk after Bykov had made the young girl pregnant (as he might have done with Varvara). This is all part of Anna Fyodorovna's business arrangements.

The work provides a glimpse of a whole line of girls being used in this lurid way—and of what was being accepted in the Russian society of the time. This evocation of a whole series of similar situations is one technique that Dostoevsky uses, and will continue to use, to increase the social density of his portrayal of Russian life. It also provides a means of varying his basic theme by contrasting different reactions to the same set of circumstances.

Young Pokrovsky is not developed very much as a character here, but he becomes a very important type in Dostoevsky's later work. He is the first of the young intellectuals who do not come from the upper class and who are called in Russian *raznochintsy*, those who have no *chin*, or rank, within the fourteen social categories, a system of classification established by Peter the Great. In a way, Devushkin can also be considered in this category, or at least aspiring to belong to it, but since he works for the bureaucracy he is still not a pure example of the type. The *raznochintsy* as a group will be distinguished by standing outside all of the ordinary structures of the established social order of life.

Even though Young Pokrovsky is not really developed here, his admiration for Pushkin, which precedes the important thematic use of Pushkin in the text, is worth noticing. The whole episode involving Varvara's and Old Pokrovsky's tremendous effort to buy the younger man, as a birthday present, an edition of Pushkin's collected works, is used to bring out the pathetic pride of the old drunkard and to show his genuine respect, in the midst of his own degradation, for the higher values of culture embodied in the son that he very well knows is not his. This is almost an epitome of the main theme of the book: the existence in someone like him, from whom you would least expect it, of genuinely fine feelings and unselfish behavior. The funeral scene in which Old Pokrovsky runs after a simple cart carrying his son's coffin, with books falling out his pockets, is sentimental, but not maudlin, and intensely moving. The critic Belinsky wrote that it was impossible not to laugh at Old Pokrovsky, "but if he does not touch you deeply at the same time you are laughing . . . do not speak of this to anyone, so that some Pokrovsky, a buffoon and a drunkard, will not have to blush for you as a human being."[2] Scenes of this kind became part of Dostoevsky's trademark as a writer, though they became subordinate to other themes later.

Poor Folk is actually much more than a series of physiological sketches of urban life and urban types because these sketches are held together by a central story. Externally, this story is that of the relationship between the two main characters, but internally it is that of the inner development of Makar Devushkin himself. He gives an account of his own life, and we see that at first, he is not unlike Gogol's hero in being proud of his work. At least on the surface, he seems content with his lot in life. In his letter of June 12, he writes that the bread he eats is his own, earned by his own labors and consumed lawfully. He knows that being a copy clerk is hardly a very honorable position, but there is nothing dishonorable about it, and it's useful. But like Gogol's Akakii Akakiyevich, he becomes the office butt, made fun of all the time by others; the difference is that he suffers from all this ridicule very deeply.

2. Belinsky's article was reprinted in *Dostoevsky v russkoi kritike* (Dostoevsky in Russian Literary Criticism) (Moscow: Goslitizdat, 1956), 16.

We can say that Dostoevsky here is developing the one scene in *The Overcoat* that appeals to Christian compassion. Dostoevsky makes Makar Devushkin both extremely self-conscious and articulate, and the reader sees the world through Devushkin's eyes, making this a worm's-eye view of the world without its appearing ridiculous; that perspective was something new in literature. And he was very conscious of presenting Devushkin in this way, as we can see in the character's letter of August 1, in which he writes that he is "a man who is poor, is overly sensitive, and he even looks at God's world differently" because he is so self-conscious that people may look down on him and regard him with contempt. Devushkin thus, at first, accepts his own world and low status, though unhappy about the way he is treated and regarded, but his negative reactions are purely personal. In his letter of July 8, Devushkin accepts the social hierarchy as God-given, but as his situation and that of Varvara become worse and worse, other feelings begin to stir inside him. And in his letter of September 5, Devushkin erupts into outright rebellion against the social inequalities he had formerly taken for granted.

These inequalities are expressed indirectly by juxtaposing (in the style of the physiological sketches of the Natural School) the dark, dank miserable streets along the canal, where he begins his walk, with the blazing lights, elegant stores, and fashionable carriages of the Nevsky Boulevard on which he emerges. Suddenly, all his grief boils up as he looks at the richly attired aristocratic ladies in the carriages and questions why Varvara, who is in no way inferior to them, is forced to suffer and endure such a wicked fate.

Generalizing his protest beyond Varvara's case, he rants against the injustices of the whole basis of the aristocratic society of the time, founded entirely on the privileges of birth, not merit. And he contrasts these wealthy aristocrats with those people who, no matter how humble, earn their living by their own efforts. De-vushkin feels that even a lowly street musician, an organ-grinder, is worthy of more respect than an aristocrat who does nothing because, at least, he earns his own pittance and supports himself. This contrast between the idle aristocrat and a street musician may initially strike the reader as just the expression of a personal frustration, with no larger significance. But in those days, and particularly in a tsarist society like Russia's, it was considered subversive and even socialistic. Devushkin's outpouring of frustration against the existing social order echoes one of the important early utopian socialists, Henri de Saint-Simon (1760–1825), who had stressed the moral superiority of work, and earning one's subsistence by the sweat of one's brow, over the aristocrats who actually were in charge of society and responsible for its inefficiency and injustices.

Devushkin thus emotionally rises in revolt against his own society, and he is very conscious of doing so. Even more, he is frightened at his own audacity and soon shrinks back from feelings that he knows are dangerous and forbidden because they violate the perfect obedience he should feel as a loyal subject and which he continues to feel with one part of his personality. He even exhibits a sense of guilt about his own thoughts and feelings, chiding himself and referring to it as "free-thinking." One of Dostoevsky's hallmarks as a writer is creating characters such as Makar Devushkin, who are caught in this kind of inner struggle between rebellious ideas and impulses and a sense of guilt. This conflict will become much more complicated later, but characters caught in this pattern of inner struggle will remain the same.

Devushkin also depicts the beggars in the streets, and since he cannot offer alms because of his own poverty, he rails against the more prosperous citizens and castigates the upper class of his own society who simply disregard the appeals made to them in the name of Christ to relieve some of the distress to which the lower class is subjected. Again, in those days, such an attack on the upper class for its lack of charity could also be seen as implicitly socialistic since Saint-Simon had called his own doctrines a "new Christianity," and the utopian socialists looked on themselves as applying the morality of charity preached by Christ to the conditions of the modern world.

Charity is also addressed in the allegorical passage about boots that follows and that is an example of what the Russians call Aesopian language—saying something indirectly and figuratively in order to get it past the censorship. The poor cobbler who has to feed his wife and children has every right to think only about boots—that is, his own immediate economic concerns. But wealthy people who live in the same building actually also think only about boots—even though they have all the money they need. Why don't they think about a more noble subject—using their wealth to relieve the misery of others? And here Devushkin follows his own advice by giving a little money to the Gorshkov family, whose misery is worse than his own. This genuine act of charity is yet another example of the kind of parallel situation that Dostoevsky uses to show various gradations of the same thematic motif.

The theme of charity is also illustrated in the letter of September 9, which describes Devushkin's encounter with the General in charge of his department. He has now reached the very bottom of humiliation, and he is terrified and rooted to his chair when summoned before his superior, feeling as if he was not even there. We will discuss it further when we look at *The Double*. There is a marked difference between the behavior of the official here and the official in Gogol's *The Overcoat*. The official in

Poor Folk is not appalled by Devushkin's threadbare appearance, by the button falling off Devushkin's jacket and bouncing along the floor (a typical Dostoevskyan detail) but, instead, he is so moved that he gives him a hundred rubles.

Even more important for Devushkin than receiving a hundred rubles is that the General shakes his hand. A handshake is no ordinary matter; it is a gesture of democratic equality, and superiors never shook hands with the lowly clerks, their inferiors. And that is why Devushkin is so overwhelmed by the General's gesture and says that the hundred rubles is less important to him than the handshake. Though the rubles are not forgotten, the emphasis is on the importance of the spiritual or psychological in the broad sense in this interchange, the treatment of the humble and humiliated inferior as a social equal.

In another scene described by Devushkin in a letter dated September 18, the practical once again is made to be subordinate—to the moral-spiritual, to the dignity of the personality. In that scene, Gorshkov, after he finally wins his lawsuit and is now entitled to a sum of money, speaks only of having his honor restored. And when the cynical writer Rataziayev pats Gorshkov on the shoulder, congratulating him on the money that he is about to receive, Devushkin writes that Gorshkov looked offended as he removed Rataziayev's hand from his shoulder. This opposition between the material and practical on the one hand, and the moral-spiritual, the needs and feelings of the human personality on the other, will later take on major significance for Dostoevsky.

It is important to mention the literary aspects of *Poor Folk*, which appear in two forms: one is through the character of Rataziayev, the hack writer, who lives in the same rooming house as Devushkin, and who is churning out manuscripts in any style that he thinks he can sell. Devushkin's initial admiration of Rataziayev and his work, which he displays in his letter of June 26, allows Dostoevsky to parody the various types of writing against which he and the other writers of the Natural School were in reaction. But there is an indirect and subtler parody of passages from the old-fashioned romantic novels, in which aristocratic characters of the highest society express undying love or burning passion of one kind or another. While the reader may be amused at Devushkin's admiration for such second-rate and old-fashioned stuff, at the same time it does present a profound contrast between the fakery of highfaluting romance and the pathetically genuine story of Devushkin himself, living out his love and caring for Varvara while sinking deeper and deeper into poverty. There is even a parody of one of Gogol's humorous stories, in preparation for the specific reference to *The Overcoat* that is yet to come.

We see Devushkin, in his letter of July 8, express his outrage at the humorously superior and condescending tone and treatment in the story and the insulting image that he sees given of someone like himself—and this reaction can be taken as partly that of Dostoevsky himself. Devushkin identifies himself completely with Akakii's humiliation, and complains that Gogol's story will now make his life harder because he will feel that everyone is now looking down on him in the same way, and no one will even think of offering him an overcoat or buying him a new pair of boots. Devushkin would like to see stories that show him in a much better light, a happy ending, with his being rewarded by his official superiors for all his virtues. While all this seems very naïve and is quite in keeping with Devushkin's character, at the same time it points to what Dostoevsky is deliberately doing here himself—that is, arousing sympathy for Devushkin in a much more sophisticated fashion that does not allow for any happy ending.

The introduction of Pushkin's story "The Stationmaster" is used to balance that of *The Overcoat*. When Devushkin reads that story he is just swept away. As he writes in his letter of July 1, he sees the sad fate of Samson Vyrin, the father in the short story, as happening not only to himself but all around him. Tears come to his eyes as he reads about the father becoming a hopeless drunkard, staving off his grief with punch, and going completely to pieces because he lost his daughter. This is quite obviously a foreshadowing of the fate that awaits Devushkin himself after he loses his "Varenka" (the diminutive, endearing form of Varvara) to Bykov, who returns to St. Petersburg and offers to marry her. Without any sense of guilt or remorse, Bykov wants Varenka to produce a child for him, an heir who would inherit his estate and keep it out of the clutches of his nephew, whom he dislikes. In view of her situation, and partly out of a sense of pity for Devushkin, for all the sacrifices that he has already made for her, she agrees to what she knows will be a life of misery, exiled in the depths of the Russian provinces, as the wife of the boorish Bykov. The book thus ends semitragically for Varvara and for the other characters as well. Gorshkov, his honor finally cleared, dies just as things seem to be getting better. And it is quite clear that Devushkin will go to rack and ruin once Varvara leaves.

The last few letters of Devushkin are of special interest because, as in the case of Gorshkov's death, they raise the theme of *Poor Folk* from a purely social-psychological level to one that deals with the more intangible issues of human life. However, this is still a very subordinate motif here, and the main theme is predominantly the social one of inequality, injustice, and humiliation. Devushkin challenged these injustices on an emotional level, but he worried at the same time that his attitude might be considered subversive free thinking. While he may not be ready emotionally to accept this existing social order passively, he mainly continues to insist that it was God-given and, therefore, not to be questioned as a whole. It is only under the impact of the impending loss of Varenka that he begins to question the wisdom of God himself. Devushkin appears to be accepting God's will, but at the same time, there is a faint note of protest heard, foreshadowing later developments in Dostoevsky's work, and in particular, this religious or metaphysical tendency will later dominate the social theme although the two will always be found together. In *Poor Folk* we have the first timid and hesitant expression of the great theme of theodicy, the questioning of the wisdom of the world created by God—thus a questioning of God himself—that will ultimately culminate in *The Brothers Karamazov*.

CHAPTER 2

The Double

Dostoevsky's next work, following immediately after the novella *Poor Folk*, was *The Double*. This novella poses a number of problems and is much more difficult to discuss than his first creation. For one thing, *The Double* was not a success when it was published and, in fact, ruined Dostoevsky's literary reputation for a time. The prominent literary and social critic Vissarion Belinsky criticized the novella very harshly, though he continued to express his admiration for Dostoevsky's talent and said that its main character, Mr. Golyadkin, belonged in a mental hospital rather than in the pages of a journal. This remark, incidentally, started a whole line of criticism that continued to haunt Dostoevsky all his life. Over and over again, picking up Belinsky's hint, critics accused Dostoevsky's characters of being pathological and not at all realistic representations of Russian life.

There is a certain amount of truth in this accusation if we compare Dostoevsky to other Russian writers of his generation, or even compare his work to the average literary novel. Indeed, Dostoevsky's characters are certainly not the usual run-of-the-mill types. Dostoevsky himself was well aware of this and defined his own approach as that of fantastic realism. He recognized that his characters were exaggerated and behaved in extreme, and what might be considered abnormal, and thus fantastic ways. But he also insisted that, in doing so, they were realistic. They were, in his view, carrying out ideas and tendencies ordinarily existing in Russian society, as it were, in a less concentrated form. Dostoevsky saw himself as taking these tendencies to their extremes and thus becoming fantastic in the process. But he did not think that he was betraying reality in doing so. In fact, quite the contrary. He thought that he was depicting the true reality underlying the routine of Russian life. He defined what he thought he was doing in a letter written many years later to one of his closest friends, after publishing his novel *The Idiot*. "I have a totally different understanding of reality and realism," he wrote, "than our novelists and critics. My idealism—is more real than their realism. God! Just to narrate sensibly what we Russians have lived through . . . in our spiritual development—yes, would not the realists shout that this is fantasy! And yet this is genuine, existing realism. This is realism, only deeper; while they swim in shallow waters." Dostoevsky thus later spoke of himself as creating a fantastic realism, which may sound like a contradiction in terms.

But while Dostoevsky did not accept Belinsky's view of *The Double* as being pathological, as time went on, in the case of *The Double*, he began to feel that some of the criticisms leveled against it were justified. It was generally thought to be too long and its style to be too reminiscent of Nikolay Gogol—not the Gogol of *The Overcoat* but of some other stories. Dostoevsky thought of rewriting it almost immediately and later reworked it entirely and published it separately. But, actually, it was only twenty years later that he included a revised version of it in a new edition of his works.

The version we read now is not the original one but this revision, which is not only shortened but also changed in format. Each chapter in the original opened with a semicomic heading summarizing its contents, a form that had begun with Cervantes's *Don Quixote*. For example, the first chapter began with this subheading: "Of how the titular councilor Golyadkin awoke. Of how he outfitted himself and set forth on his appointed way. Of how he tried to justify himself in his own eyes, and of how he then figured out that it was best to be brave and frank but with a certain amount of dignity. And of where Mr. Golyadkin finally ended up." The novella was also given a new subtitle, *A Petersburg Poem*, to replace the original one, *The Adventures of Mr. Golyadkin*.

The aim of these changes, as well as others, was to minimize as much as possible the mock-heroic framework and the semi-comic atmosphere that it created. Dostoevsky obviously felt a certain incongruity with this admixture of comic elements in the story, and the new subtitle gave it a particular coloring. The adventures of Mr. Golyadkin were really part of the life that St. Petersburg (Russia's capital in the eighteenth and nineteenth centuries), with its struggle for position and power, had come to symbolize in Russian culture.

Thirteen years after the novella's original publication, Dostoevsky returned again to comment on it in a letter written in 1859, to say that the character type he created in this work was a magnificent type in terms of its social importance. Twenty years later, in his *Diary of a Writer*, Dostoevsky referred to *The Double* once more. On the one hand, he wrote that "never in literature did I pursue an idea as important as this one" that is, the idea of *The Double*. But then he added, "I failed completely when it comes to the form of the story." He never explained what he meant by this latter phrase "the form of the story," but we shall see what I think is a plausible suggestion after examining the work in a little more detail.

Just as *Poor Folk* picks up and reworks Gogol's *The Overcoat*, so *The Double* can be linked to two other stories of Gogol that unite the basic theme of repressed ambition with madness in the one case and sheer fantastic tomfoolery in the other (though it also makes a couple of social points). The first story, *Memoirs* (or *Diary*) *of a Madman*, is a little gem, with the special mixture of sadly pathetic humor, of "laughter through tears," to quote A. S. Pushkin,[1] that is one of the characteristics of Gogol's genius. The main character is another of the civil-service clerks, of the same rank as Dostoevsky's Makar Devushkin (*Poor Folk*), who falls in love with the daughter of the head of his department. The story is constructed as a series of entries in his diary, which shows the protagonist gradually losing his mind, or having already lost his mind, and the reader follows the gradual worsening of his mental condition.

Included in the diary are letters allegedly written between two dogs, one of which belongs to the lady in question. As Golyadkin learns from these letters of her attraction to a much more eligible suitor, the protagonist imagines himself rising in rank. Finally, he convinces himself that he is the king of Spain, having read in the newspapers that the throne is temporarily vacant. At first he thinks that the cruel treatment he receives in the asylum where he ends up is really his coronation, but he ends up piteously calling for his mother. The reader sees the trivial events in his ordinary life through the fantasies of his distortions, which makes the story a little masterpiece.

The other Gogol story, *The Nose*, contains much less pathos and is more overtly satirical and humorous. It concerns, once again, a lower-rank but very pretentious official who wakes up

---

1. Pushkin's expression "laughter through tears" was used in a review of the second edition of Gogol's *Evenings on a Farm Near Dikanka*; published in the journal *Sovremennik*, issue 1, 1836. In V. V. Gippius, *Gogol* [1924], ed. Robert A. Maguire (Ann Arbor, MI: Ardis, 1981).

one morning to find his nose missing. The story itself begins with a nose turning up in the breakfast rolls at the home of the barber who shaves regularly the protagonist. The poor official, who likes to be called Major (instead of his equivalent civil-service title), wanders through the streets and sees his nose, dressed in the uniform of a much higher rank, making courtesy calls on various people. When the Major tries to reclaim his nose, he is sent packing in no uncertain terms, and he then places an advertisement in a newspaper asking for its return. There are a number of other such episodes, all of them very amusing, and all of them illustrating how the loss of the nose interferes with the Major's plans to rise up the social ladder and prevents him from becoming the General that his nose has become. He finally gets his nose back, but the narrator ends by admitting that all this is so confusing that he does not even know how it happened himself.

The Double thus fits into this Russian literary tradition of what came to be known as Russian Hoffmannism, that is, writers influenced by the German Romantic writer E.T.A. Hoffmann.[2] In Hoffmann's works, "doubles" often appeared, and the fantastic created an atmosphere of supernatural mystery. Hoffmann enjoyed an enormous vogue everywhere and also influenced American literature through Edgar Allan Poe, who used the motif of the double in a story entitled "William Wilson." Before becoming converted to realism, Belinsky even declared Hoffmann to be greater than Shakespeare. Dostoevsky boasted of having read all of Hoffmann's works while still studying in the military academy and much later, in 1861, compared Hoffmann

2. E.T.A. Hoffman (1776–1822), a German Romantic author, musician, and jurist. His stories, combining elements of reality, imagination, and horror, are told in a realistic narrative style. The ballets *The Nutcracker* and *Coppelia* are also based on his stories.

and Poe, suggesting that Hoffmann was a greater writer than Poe because through his use of the fantastic he had opened up the realm of the ideal.[3] The same could be said about Dostoevsky, although his form of fantastic usually stayed closer to the ordinary world.

One of the best Russian literary critics, Victor Vladimirovich Vinogradov, said that *The Double* consists of "a naturalistic transformation of the Romantic 'doubles' of Russian Hoffmannism" into the very unromantic environment of the Russian bureaucratic world, thus continuing in the footsteps of Gogol. But *The Double* is, moreover, also a transformation of these Romantic doubles into the social psychology of characters already created in such a figure as Devushkin. Particular attention should be paid to the passage in *Poor Folk* when Devushkin is called into the office of the head of his department. More frightened than he had ever been in his life, his panic-stricken reaction was to pretend he wasn't himself. Devushkin wishes to vanish as he is and to become someone else. In *The Double*, an identical reaction leads to the actual splitting of Golyadkin's personality and the appearance of his double. The same sort of terror causes him to wish to be someone else—but this time, someone who succeeds in obtaining everything that the real Golyadkin is denied. At the same time, Golyadkin feels guilty at harboring such desires because they are an implicit revolt against the established social order.

Although Golyadkin comes from the same social milieu as Devushkin, there is a considerable difference in their individual

3. Fyodor Dostoevsky, preface to publication of "Three Stories by Edgar Poe," in F. M. Dostoevskii, *Polnoe sobranie sochinenii v tridtsati tomakh*, ed. V. G. Bazanov et al. (Moscow: SPb Nauka), vol. 15. The preface originally appeared in the journal *Vremia*, vol. 11, in 1861.

characters. Devushkin's sinking into poverty and desperation is a result of trying to help Varvara, and he feels pity for the Gorshkovs, who are even worse off than himself. He, too, dreams of becoming something else and rising higher in the social scale, but these ambitions are more literary and cultural and are not concerned with his bureaucratic career. And although he genuinely loves Varvara, he knows that the difference in their ages makes impossible any hope of a relationship other than friendship. Golyadkin, on the other hand, aspires to the hand of Klara, the daughter of the head of his department, although he hardly knows her at all. There is no indication that he values her for anything except her coveted social status.

Also, there is nothing charitable or self-sacrificing about Golyadkin, who is financially much better off than Devushkin. The reader is shown how carefully Golyadkin looks after his money. One of the first things he does on getting up on the morning the story begins is to examine his savings with extreme pleasure. He is not impoverished and lives in his own flat with his own man-servant, Petrushka. As assistant to the chief clerk in his office, he is thus also a step higher in the bureaucratic hierarchy. Conceivably, it is this higher status that ultimately leads to his own downfall because it motivates him to rise even higher and thereby violate the rules of the social hierarchy within which he exists by questioning the authority of his superiors. Here Dostoevsky breaks the connection established earlier between Devushkin's poverty and his struggle for recognition and self-respect. This latter motif takes over in *The Double* but in such a form that it's difficult to sympathize with it as a struggle against social injustice. And this is why the critic Vissarion Belinsky called the story "pathological," since Golyadkin can well be seen as having brought all his troubles on himself by being overly ambitious.

A year after writing *The Double*, Dostoevsky printed an article that, without mentioning the story explicitly, helps us to better understand the type of character he was trying to create in Golyadkin. This article describes what happens to various types of people who are unable to fulfill their egos in real life, and it lists various kinds of aberrant behavior that result. One such type is a person who "goes off his head because of ambition, at the same time completely despising ambition and even suffering because he has had to suffer over such nonsense as ambition." The English word "ambition" translates a similar word in Russian "амбиция, *ambitsia*," and while the English word is more or less morally neutral or even indicates a positive characteristic (there's nothing wrong with being "ambitious" in English), in the Russian language it bears a negative connotation. It tends to mean that one is aspiring to something to which one is not really entitled. So Golyadkin is ambitious while despising ambition at the same time; the focus of the story is thus on this inner conflict and the problems it creates.

The first several chapters of *The Double* give a brilliant picture of the gradually developing split in Golyadkin's personality before it breaks into two separate entities. On the one hand, we see his obvious and ludicrous desire to pretend to a higher social station and a more flattering image of himself. He is clearly living in the world of his desires, and not in reality, when he hires a carriage and livery to ape the style of his social superiors. Then he goes shopping as if he were on the point of being married and had already been accepted as the future husband of Klara, though of course all this is a total fantasy. In a brilliant detail, he is even shown to have changed his banknotes into smaller denominations, so his wallet will look fatter.

With one part of his personality, he nourishes this sense of self-delusion. But with another, he is terrified at his own audacity and shrinks back when he has to confront others who know him for what he really is. When he sees the two clerks from his office as he is riding along in his carriage, he hides from their sight. And when he catches sight of his office head, Andrey Filippovich, he has the same reaction already noted in the case of Devushkin: "To bow down or not? To respond or not? . . . or to just pretend that it's not me but someone else who is a spitting image of me, and just pretend nothing is the matter? Not me, not me indeed, and that's all!" (chapter 1). But then Golyadkin summons up his courage again (or tries to do so), and the narrator speaks ironically of him, "glaring defiantly at the front corner of the carriage with the sole purpose of reducing all his foes to ashes at once." From the tone, the reader can guess how little defiance Golyadkin actually projects and how little effect it has on his perceived foes.

Dostoevsky follows his usual technique here of beginning a work in the middle, as it were, and then revealing the origins of the situation either in flashbacks (as he does in later novels) or, as here, by Golyadkin's medical visit. Golyadkin's behavior dramatizes all his indecision and the origins of his strange comportment. He has been passed over for promotion, in his view unjustly, and has made clear, even if indirectly, that he resents the favoritism that Andrey Filippovich has shown to his nephew. Along with the position, the nephew also gets the girl, Klara, though it is very unlikely that she ever had any interest in Golyadkin in the first place. What becomes clear, in the conversation with the doctor, is that Golyadkin is terrified at his own audacity but still refuses to admit to himself that his behavior has placed him in an impossible situation. This is illustrated when he tries to gain admittance to the party to which he has deliberately *not* been invited—and is then insultingly refused entrance. But he sneaks in, and the pages depicting Golyadkin's state of mind while standing in the hallway closet are brilliantly done. Here we see the narrator sinking into the consciousness of the character, as it were, in a manner that will become characteristic—and later, problematic—for Dostoevsky, though in this case doing so very ironically.

It is worth focusing on the description of Klara's birthday party: it is hyperbolic to such an extent that, of course, the reader knows that it means the very opposite of what it says. These bureaucrats are just unsuccessfully trying to imitate the manners of genuine high society, and everything said about them indicates that their milieu is a hotbed of bribe-taking and corruption. About Klara's father, for example, the narrator describes as someone whom "... destiny has rewarded him with a pot of money, a house, a few villages, and a beautiful daughter." (*The Double*, chapter 4)

Leaving out the beautiful daughter, every Russian reader would understand that such prosperity, in a civil servant, came from taking bribes. As for the rival of Golyadkin, Vladimir Semyonovich, he "practically spelled out, so to speak, that good manners can lead to this kind of high standing!" (chapter 4). But we know that the nephew obtained promotion only through nepotism and that such praise is the very opposite of the truth. Compared to such successful rascals, poor Golyadkin, who had believed that his devotion to duty would get him somewhere, does not appear in too bad a light.

It is after his ignominious eviction from the party that Golyadkin's double finally appears. Dostoevsky prepares the reader for this appearance with a virtuoso passage about St. Petersburg and the storm written in the style of the historical novel: "All the clocks on St. Petersburg's clock towers had just struck midnight" (*The Double*, chapter 5). But more important is the depiction of Golyadkin's state of mind, which has reached the very nadir of despair: "he not only wished to run away from himself but to obliterate himself completely, cease to exist, return to dust" (*The Double*, chapter 8). It is under these circumstances that the double finally manifests itself, as if in response to this desire and to these feelings. Golyadkin does become somebody else who is identical in outward figure but of an entirely different type of personality. The two sides of his character, his ambition on the one hand and the fear induced by exhibiting such ambition on the other, become split in two.

The first five chapters of *The Double* showed Golyadkin trying to assert himself in the real world. In the remainder of the work, we see him carrying on an unsuccessful struggle to keep from being replaced by his double, who knows how to achieve the success that the real Golyadkin was never able to obtain. At first, Golyadkin's double is obsequious, deferential, ingratiating, and it is he who even begs Golyadkin for protection. This behavior is probably meant to be a flashback to the start of Golyadkin's own career, when he was struggling out of poverty and humiliation and must have behaved in this way to people like the head of his department, Andrey Filippovich. But once the double has wormed his way into Golyadkin's confidence and learns all his secrets, he then "betrays" him just as Golyadkin himself is betraying his superiors by his own insubordination. The double thus represents all those aspects of Golyadkin that he has been trying to suppress in himself because he knows that they are against the societal rules; ultimately, however, he is unable to control his ambitions.

It is in this latter part of the work that Golyadkin tries to prove that he is a docile and obedient subordinate, while his double gets ahead by trickery and deception. What bothers Golyadkin the most is that he might be confused with his double, that the authorities will make no distinction between them, and that his own virtues will go unrecognized. For while the double is a rascal and a scoundrel, Golyadkin is "honest, virtuous, meek, placable, quite reliable when it came to work, and worthy of advancement to a higher rank . . . but what if . . . but what if they get us mixed up?!" What if his own virtues go unrecognized? What if the authorities make no distinction between the two of them? The more Golyadkin is abused and humiliated by his double, the more he appeals to his superiors and throws himself on their mercy. In a famous passage suggesting Dostoevsky's own social sympathy for the downtrodden, Golyadkin feels that because of his double, he himself is being reduced to a rag, even "this old milksop would have had ambitions, the milksop would've had a heart and feelings, and even though if ambition and feelings were unrequited, all the same, hidden deep inside this rag of a person's dirty folds, it would have had them" (chapter 8).

Golyadkin enters a world of self-deception similar to that of Gogol's madman, and the final scenes, involving the delusion of being romantically involved with Klara and exchanging letters with her, are a parody of the sentimental romantic novel. One of the most amusing parts of the novella, which provides a relief from the continual punishment to which Golyadkin is exposed, is found in these final chapters. Here, his own seesaw between obedience and rebellion is transferred to his relation with Klara, and he rebukes her mentally, both for disobeying the rules of good behavior prescribed for young maidens and at the same time for agreeing to run away with him. The novella ends with a touching scene in which Golyadkin is led by his double into the house from which he had previously been evicted. Suddenly, everybody seems very friendly. He now feels reconciled with man and destiny, and "could distinctly feel the hot tears coursing down his cheeks" (*The Double*, chapter 13). But, of course, they are all only waiting for the arrival of Dr. Rutenspitz, who is coming to take Golyadkin away to an insane asylum. He leaves, escorted by his double and the doctor, and then he loses consciousness. When he awakens, he sees Dr. Rutenspitz in the form of a devil who now speaks with a German accent and drives home his own sense of guilt by telling him that he does not deserve even the minimal care he is about to receive.

The novella, even in its rewritten, shortened form, is still somewhat repetitious, but the portrayal of Golyadkin's bewildered consciousness is brilliantly done and displays Dostoevsky's talent for psychological portraiture. However, Dostoevsky himself thought the work a failure because of its form, although he provided no further explanation. In an attempt to understand his harsh judgment, I should like to offer my own explanation of what I think he meant.

If we go back to chapter 5, to the point at which the double appears to Golyadkin, there can hardly be any doubt that his origin is psychological and that the double represents those aspects of Golyadkin's personality that the latter had been trying to suppress. By breaking all the rules of proper behavior, the double obtains the success that Golyadkin thinks he himself deserves and of which he has been unfairly deprived. The double objectifies, as it were, the subconscious and illegitimate desires (in terms of the prevalent social system) that Golyadkin has been trying to suppress. The double thus seems to exist as a projection of Golyadkin's psyche and reaches his deepest significance only when seen in this way.

However, Dostoevsky gives the double another origin as well. It seems as if the double also exists in the story quite independent of the consciousness of Golyadkin because he is observed by at least one other character in the text. This is Golyadkin's bureau chief, and he and Golyadkin carry on a conversation about the oddity of nature in producing two people who look exactly alike and work in the same office. This second, "visible" double undercuts and weakens the significance of the first—namely, the projection of the struggle in the psyche of Golyadkin—and the most important aspect of the work thus tends to be lost.

The second, visible double is used primarily for external comic effect, as it was in *The Nose*, thereby again weakening the seriousness of the conflict that Dostoevsky wishes to convey. One could argue that Dostoevsky, at this point, was still too much under the influence of Gogol, imitating his playfulness and avoiding psychological probing. It is worth noting that when Dostoevsky, in his later work, did use the technique of the double again, those doubles always appeared only as a dream or an hallucination—that is, strictly as a psychological projection.

Whatever the weakness of its form, though, Dostoevsky also said that the idea embodied in *The Double* was more serious than anything else he had contributed to Russian literature.[4] Without further explanation on his part, we can only speculate about his meaning—namely, that when he spoke of his idea, he actually meant the character type of Golyadkin, a figure struggling unsuccessfully to suppress in himself aspects of his personality that he is unwilling to face. He is caught in an inner

---

4. "Most decidedly, I did not succeed with that novel; however, its idea was rather lucid, and I have never expressed in my writings anything more serious. Still, as far as form was concerned, I failed utterly" [12]. Fyodor Dostoevsky, "The History of the Verb 'Stushevatsia'" in *Diary of a Writer*, trans. Boris Brasol (New York: Octagon Books, 1973), 2: 882–85.

conflict between obedience to a repressive external authority and his own ambitions, which here, admittedly, are not very exalting, but this type of inner conflict provides a psychological pattern to be filled in later with more important and elevated alternatives.

Authority in Dostoevsky's later work will no longer be externally repressive. Instead, it will be identified as embodied in the European ideas that were affecting the Russian intelligentsia. For the educated classes were now caught in an inner struggle caused by the disintegrating effect of the atheistic radical ideology imported from European culture. As Dostoevsky saw it, these ideas came into conflict with the innately moral-religious Russian national character; and this meant the continuing conflict of Christian moral conscience with ideas. We already saw the beginning of this kind of inner conflict between morality and rebellion in Devushkin—and on a much larger scale in Golyadkin. Even though the cause of this type of conflict changed, Dostoevsky could already foresee the ultimate importance of his new character type.

While everybody recognized the psychological power of Dostoevsky's portrayal of Golyadkin, the novella was a flop for several reasons: first, it was too long, as Dostoevsky recognized himself by shortening it later; second, many features of the novella seemed too imitative of Gogol. Andrey Biely, a great twentieth-century Russian writer, called it "a patchwork quilt stitched together from the subjects, gestures and verbal procedures of Gogol."[5] And ultimately, readers found uninteresting and boring all of the irrelevant and nonsensical references and allusions floating through Golyadkin's agitated

---

5. Joseph Frank, *Dostoevsky: The Seeds of Revolt* (Princeton, NJ: Princeton University Press, 1976), 308.

consciousness. The readers were perhaps not yet ready for stream-of-consciousness technique.

But the most important reason of all for the response was the inability on the part of readers to identify with the protagonists. While Devushkin, in *Poor Folk*, was sacrificing himself for Varvara, who was herself a victim of the injustices of the system, it was very easy for the reader to sympathize with them. In *The Double*, however, Golyadkin is not suffering from poverty and shows no concern for others at all. He has been treated unfairly and is thus also a victim, but what he desires has no moral substance—he simply wants to rise a bit higher in the social hierarchy, which, in fact, is shown by the irony of the narrator to be totally corrupt.

It is thus difficult for the reader to feel any sympathy for Golyadkin since he does not represent anything worthier than those by whom he is being oppressed. Indeed, according to the critic Belinsky, Golyadkin's life would have been bearable except "for the unhealthy susceptibility and suspiciousness of his character."[6] Moreover, Belinsky believed that Golyadkin was himself to blame for his problems and that his sufferings did not seem to make any social point. His view is not entirely justified because Dostoevsky does indicate certain features of Golyadkin that might be taken as positive. Unlike his colleagues, he is not a hypocrite or a scoundrel. With one side of his personality, he genuinely believes in the rightness and goodness of the social order in which he lives. He genuinely believes that virtue will be rewarded, and in this sense he may be considered naïve but not really corrupt like everyone else. And he continues to believe so, while his double shows that he subconsciously knows all this to be a delusive fiction. It is the conflict between the two that finally

6. Ibid., 309.

drives Golyadkin mad. But by internalizing the protagonist's conflict so completely, Dostoevsky creates a special problem for the reader.

In other works that Dostoevsky wrote during the 1840s, the same process of internalization is taking place. And even much later, in the 1860s, somewhat the same problem as in *The Double* arises in *Notes from Underground*. By expressing his ideological theme only through the psychology of his narrator, Dostoevsky makes it very difficult to grasp his own point of view.

CHAPTER 3

The House of the Dead

Lecture 1

Dostoevsky's next work is only semifictional, in the sense that everything and everybody he writes about (with the single exception of a frame-narrator) actually existed. The book is what might be called a semiautobiography, describing his experiences in the prison camp where he served four years and lived cheek by jowl with all the peasant prisoners that he describes. This book was written fifteen years after *The Double*, and the experiences of these years marked an important turning point in Dostoevsky's life, both intellectually and spiritually. He realized this himself and later wrote of this stretch of time as having marked "the regeneration of his convictions."[1] The meaning of this phrase has been interpreted in a variety of ways by those writing about Dostoevsky.

First, we need to take a closer look at why Dostoevsky was arrested in the first place. He belonged to the Petrashevsky circle, a group of utopian socialists who got together once a week at the home of a man named Mikhail Butashevich-Petrashevsky to discuss the problems of the day. Petrashevsky was the same age as Dostoevsky, and he had a post in the ministry of foreign affairs

1. Fyodor Dostoevsky, *A Writer's Diary, Vol. 1: 1873–1876*, trans. Kenneth Lantz (Evanston, IL: Northwestern University Press, 1997).

as a translator. There was nothing secret or illegal about this group, though they discussed social problems that the Russian authorities thought should better have been left untouched. The Russian secret police had infiltrated these gatherings, and the circle was finally arrested for engaging in this sort of subversive talk because the revolutions breaking out all over Europe in 1848 had led to a tightening of controls over public opinion. Of course, this opinion was that of only a small handful of people, what is now called the Russian intelligentsia. The vast majority of the Russian population was peasant serfs, most of whom were illiterate.

The Petrashevsky circle, or the *Petrashevtsy*, as a whole was a perfectly harmless group and had no revolutionary inclinations at all. The utopian socialists of the pre-1848 period, before the rise of Marxism (the "Communist Manifesto" was published in 1848), did not believe in class warfare or attempting to improve the lot of the lower classes by force and violence. What they wished to do was to reform society peacefully by example and bring it closer to the morality of love and charity preached by Christ. Petrashevsky himself was a follower of Fourier, who had built on his own small estate an example of the ideal community that Fourier called a "phalanstery," a cooperative communal structure where people would live and work together for their mutual benefit. But the day after it was built, the peasants burned it to the ground. All the same, Petrashevsky continued to believe in the merits of Fourier's ideas and in the social morality that Dostoevsky had already learned about through the newer French writers such as George Sand, a female author who wrote under a male pseudonym and whom he continued to admire all his life. The same morality was expressed in *Poor Folk*, with its plea to the richer class to think about others and its portrait of the charitable General. Utopian socialism thus had a strong Christian component, and, in a certain sense, this aspect of socialism remained with Dostoevsky all his life.

Dostoevsky was thus strongly affected by the idea of applying this Christian concept of love and charity to the problems of ordinary daily social life. But he did not accept, on the other hand, any of the numerous plans proposed by various socialist thinkers for reorganizing social life entirely to attain this objective. Such thinkers were called utopians because each had worked out some plan for reconstructing social life from top to bottom in order to attain an ideal society. So far as we know, Dostoevsky did not accept any of these blueprints because they infringed too much on the freedom of the individual. And although at this period of his life such an emphasis on the freedom of the individual was only a theoretical conviction, it exemplified Dostoevsky's wariness about accepting any of the plans for the communal organization of social life advocated by any of the utopian socialist thinkers. We shall see later that Dostoevsky's concern for the freedom of the individual personality, already in evidence here, became very important when he actually experienced communal life in prison.

Even though Dostoevsky can be seen as a kind of Christian socialist, who accepted the ideals of socialism, if not any specific plan, we now know that shortly before being arrested, he had joined a genuine conspiracy aimed at stirring up revolution. How can this inconsistency be explained?

First, we may want to look at the kind of revolution that the conspirators had in mind. Their major aim was the abolition of serfdom, that is, the system that reduced the vast majority of the peasant population to the status of slaves. Russia was the only European country in which this relic of the Middle Ages continued to exist (although slavery also existed at that time, we should remember, in the southern part of the United States).

Dostoevsky took very little part in the discussions that were carried on in the Petrashevsky circle and only spoke two or three times. When he did so, it was always to denounce the injustices of serfdom, and he did it with such passion that his vehemence was remarked upon by others. He was always so much carried away by emotion that it may help to understand why he joined this revolutionary group. And this emotion may have derived from the rumors that could have reached his ears about the possible murder of his father by his peasants—though evidence that he believed his father to have been murdered remains very circumstantial.

The inconsistency of his behavior, as a utopian socialist advocating revolution, can also be given a larger meaning. So far as we can judge, he was by conviction a Christian socialist believing in a morality of charity and love. But to rectify a glaring social injustice he could not bear, he consented to the use of violence and bloodshed as a remedy. In fact, his conspiracy never got off the ground (luckily for the future of Russian literature). The point, however, is that Dostoevsky could understand how someone, starting with the highest idealism and the finest moral principles as ends, could agree to accomplish such ends through the use of the most ruthless and murderous means. This gave him the insight to create such a character as Raskolnikov in *Crime and Punishment*, for example. It also colored his attitude toward the radicals, with whom he later disagreed, but whom he could never consider to be morally evil and malignant.

It also helps to explain something that has bothered a number of biographers, who have noted his later lack of resentment at his prison sentence, especially since he seems to have been guilty of nothing but subversive talk. This has also led to all sorts of theories about his masochistic character. But if we remember that he knew he was guilty of something far more serious, which, if discovered, might have led to a much more severe sentence, we can understand why he later seemed to feel that he had not suffered any severe injustice in being sent to prison. Another question that arises at this point is to clarify just what it meant to be a Christian socialist at this period. It meant to believe in the morality of love and self-sacrifice that came from Christianity. But to what extent did it also mean that Dostoevsky believed in other tenets of the Christian faith, such as Christ's supernatural origins and powers? It is important to understand just what Dostoevsky's convictions were at this crucial moment of his life. His own writing seems ambiguous on this issue and may have only contributed to further misunderstanding. I will try to explain why and what I believe the true picture to be.

One of the most important influences on Dostoevsky's early literary career, as already mentioned, was Vissarion Belinsky, the prominent social and literary critic and publicist. Belinsky underwent a complicated ideological evolution, and 1845, the year he met Dostoevsky, was a transition period in his own development. In the early 1840s he had become converted to French utopian socialism, which rejected many of the theological doctrines of the official churches but still accepted the divinity of Christ. But just at this time another current of socialist thought, coming from Germany, began to compete with the French ideas everywhere in Europe. This was Ludwig Feuerbach's book *The Essence of Christianity*, which exercised an enormous influence all over Europe and was translated into English by no less than the great novelist George Eliot. It was also translated into Russian and circulated underground. The book created a huge furor because it undermined the relation that had existed until then between Christianity and social radicalism.

Feuerbach was a philosopher belonging to a group called the Left Hegelians, that is, those who interpreted and extended Hegel's ideas, which were dominant at that time in European thought, so as to give them a radical and revolutionary character. Karl Marx also emerged out of this group.[2] In *The Essence of Christianity*, which is not a polemic but a serious theological study, Feuerbach interpreted the doctrines and dogmas of Christianity not as supernatural truths but as projections of mankind's highest ideals. These truths had been placed in some transcendental realm and, supposedly, given to mankind by God, when in fact they were creations of mankind itself. By locating these highest ideals in God and Christ, mankind was thus alienating its own essence and neglecting the possibility of realizing these ideals on earth. This is why Karl Marx called religion "the opium of the people," seeing it as a drug that helped to keep them in chains and being thus the major obstacle to human progress.

Sometime in 1845, around the time he met Dostoevsky, Belinsky began to come under the influence of these ideas, and we know that the two discussed these matters very seriously. In these early years Dostoevsky accepted all of Belinsky's ideas. This led to the view that Dostoevsky had accepted the atheism of Belinsky and returned to faith only as a result of the hardships of his prison years. But in fact, the picture is more complicated.

If we look at Dostoevsky's life in this period, we see that he quarreled with the increasingly radical Belinsky in the middle of 1846. The reasons are mostly literary, but there is some evidence that the quarrel was also caused because Dostoevsky refused to

---

2. To learn more about the Left Hegelians and their importance, see Karl Löwith, *From Hegel to Nietzsche*, trans. David E. Green (New York: Columbia University Press, 1964).

accept atheism.[3] But after his quarrel with Belinsky, Dostoevsky joined another discussion circle that was also a utopian socialist group clinging to its initial French religious inspiration. This indicated that Belinsky had not succeeded in converting Dostoevsky to atheism. The same is true of the Petrashevsky circle, whose members were largely followers of Fourier's philosophy. In other words, Dostoevsky was still a religious radical at the time of his arrest. The issue is important for our understanding of what occurred to Dostoevsky just before he went off to prison camp.

After six months in solitary confinement inside Peter and Paul Fortress in St. Petersburg, during which he wrote a charming short story called "A Little Hero" that seems totally untouched by what he was going through (maybe he wrote the work to forget about his actual surroundings), Dostoevsky, along with all the other members of the Petrashevsky circle, were taken out to a large square in the city used as a parade ground. There they learned that they had all been sentenced to death and were lined up on a platform. Three were tied to stakes and blindfolded while a firing squad took its place before them. Dostoevsky was next in line, and though he never described any of this, he used some of his feelings at that time in a scene of The Idiot that will be discussed when we come to that novel.

From other descriptions, we know that everything had been arranged as if a genuine execution were to take place. A cart with coffins could be seen on the side, and a priest came carrying a cross, which they all kissed; some made confessions. The order

3. In an article he wrote thirty years later, Dostoevsky said: "I found him a passionate Socialist, and he began immediately with me on atheism." Joseph Frank, Dostoevsky: Seeds of Revolt, 1821–1849 (Princeton, NJ: Princeton University Press, 1976), 192.

was given to raise the rifles, and this was done; but then the drums of the regiment surrounding the square began to beat retreat. As an ex-army officer, Dostoevsky knew what this meant— that the execution would not take place; but while the ceremonies were going on, he and all the others believed they would die in the coming half hour or so. A messenger then arrived on horseback carrying the true sentences, and nobody was executed.

Except for the passage in *The Idiot,* and some remarks Dostoevsky made thirty years later, the most revealing information about this moment is given in a memoir written by someone who had been standing next to Dostoevsky on the platform, supposedly also awaiting execution. He mentions that Dostoevsky spoke about a story of Victor Hugo, "Le dernier jour d'un condamné" (The Last Day of a Condemned Man), which is the diary of someone awaiting execution. The story itself is a protest against capital punishment and had made a great impression on Dostoevsky.

But the most important detail is an exchange of remarks with someone named Nikolay Speshnev, who was the chief organizer of the revolutionary group of which Dostoevsky was a member. Although Speshnev was known as a Communist and an atheist, Dostoevsky said to him, speaking in French: *Nous serons avec le Christ* (we shall be with Christ). Speshnev smiled, pointed to the ground, and said: *Un peu de poussière* (a handful of dust). If someone had tried to invent an exchange of words illustrating the point I have been trying to make, he could not have done better. For this indicates that Dostoevsky did not think of death as the total end of any kind of existence but as the transition to some other realm corresponding to Christ's promise of immortality for those who believed in him. He was thus still a Christian and not an atheist.

Just after returning to prison from this harrowing event, Dostoevsky wrote a letter to his older brother Mikhail. This letter is a remarkable document that has not received sufficient attention. If there is any moment in Dostoevsky's life that can be called crucial, one that marked an epochal instant determining much of his future development, then it is this experience of the mock execution. This letter, which records Dostoevsky's immediate reaction to these events, marks the beginning of the change that took place in Dostoevsky's values and his sense of life. It is this change that accounts for some of the differences between his earlier works of the 1840s and the later works of the 1860s.

Just how to characterize these differences in some comprehensible way is not easy. It involves a shift between the foreground and the background of what we saw in the stories. The early works were dominated by the problems of the ordinary world of social experience and of society. In protesting against them, occasional references were made to God as the creator of all things, but these were very secondary and, in *The Double*, even partly comic (God creating two people exactly alike, for example). What occurs later is that this religious or metaphysical perspective moves much more into the foreground. Social conflicts continue to exist on the plot level, but now they are projected in a way that is not only primarily social.

In *Poor Folk*, Makar Devushkin for one moment comes close to accusing God for allowing Varvara to vanish from his life. But this is just a momentary flare-up that has little importance for the main theme of the work. But later, this sort of interweaving of the personal, the social, and the religious takes on much more importance. As a result, the atmosphere of Dostoevsky's later novels is often compared to that of poetic tragedy, where such an intermixture of the social and the religious is much more common than it is in the novel. If we are to look at the history of the novel, we see that it was more or less created in opposition to poetic tragedy. Its aim was to dramatize the more mundane and quotidian aspects of human life. But Dostoevsky manages to raise these events to the level of tragedy by placing them in what I call an eschatological perspective. Eschatology is a theological term meaning the doctrine of last things—death, immortality, resurrection, etc. Such preoccupations moved into the foreground for Dostoevsky because, it seems, after his experience in facing death, he could never again portray human life except in relation to these ultimate values and the ultimate choices that one becomes aware of in such moments of crisis.

We need to look at the letter that Dostoevsky wrote to his brother a little more closely to see what it reveals about his feelings. One thing of great importance is a sense of the infinite value of life in itself, quite aside from all the circumstances that condition it and from which (as he wrote on his way to prison camp) he knows he may have to suffer. But now his whole relation to outward life has changed. "Life is life everywhere," he says. "Life is inside ourselves, not in things external."[4] We have already seen how he had shifted from the poverty of Devushkin to the more internal and psychological conflict of Golyadkin. And we see here how this shift, already evident in his work, now becomes a positive principle that downgrades the importance of the material and the external. Nothing will arouse more opposition later from the post-Siberian Dostoevsky than the notion that human behavior should be judged and evaluated, and

4. From Dostoevsky's letter of December 22, 1849, to his brother M. M. Dostoevsky, written from Peter and Paul Fortress, St. Petersburg, in which he describes his death sentence, preparation for execution, and the sudden, last-minute reversal of his sentence. In F. M. Dostoevskii, *Polnoe sobranie sochinenii v tridtsati tomakh*, ed. V. G. Bazanov et al. (Moscow: SPb Nauka, 1985), 28: 164.

particularly excused, as a consequence of the effect of the surrounding material circumstances (the environment). We will see this particularly clearly when we come to his novel *Crime and Punishment*.

In another passage of the letter to his brother, he defines the ecstatic sense of life that he felt on being pardoned: "Life is a gift, life is happiness, every minute could be a lifetime of happiness." Dostoevsky's resilience and buoyancy during his lifetime, despite often living in poverty and being afflicted by epilepsy, probably can be traced at least in part to this feeling that simply being alive was something for which one should be thankful. But more central is the emphasis on the importance of the immediate moment, the feeling that every minute of life had an immense value that could be turned into "a lifetime of happiness," or, of course, its opposite. Mankind was thus continually faced with this sort of absolute choice, and this helps to explain why Dostoevsky's major characters are always in crisis situations in which such choices have to be made. His characters live for the most part in this state of eschatological apprehension, which conditions how they are seen and perceived and the sort of world that Dostoevsky depicts. In this world of eschatological apprehension, every instant takes on a supreme value. Temporal continuity, the time of historical reality and development, has little importance. Each moment of the present is when a decisive choice has to be made, and so for someone who feels this way, long-range social plans, revolutionary ideals for a future humanity would have no significance. It would be the same with individual moral behavior. What would be essential is action at every moment, at this very instant, as if time were about to stop and the world come to an end. And such action would be similar to what is expressed in Dostoevsky's letter to his brother: "There is no bitterness or rancor in my heart; I wish I could have embraced and shown love toward anyone from my past. It was joy, and I experienced it today as I was saying good-bye to my dearest ones before dying." What results is thus a feeling of a need for mutual love and forgiveness.

One way of looking at such a state of mind, and of broadening it into more than a purely personal reaction of Dostoevsky's to a particular experience, is to compare it with that of the early Christians. They too lived in a similar state of fear and hope, a similar state of eschatological apprehension, because they believed that the second coming of Christ was near at hand and could arrive on any day. This would mean both death and the end of the world but also the hope of resurrection and the transformation into an unknown heavenly existence for those not condemned to hell. In a famous book by Albert Schweitzer, *The Quest for the Historical Jesus* (published in 1907), he stresses the importance of this eschatological conviction for the formation of Christian ethics.

Schweitzer argued that Christian ethics is this kind of interim ethics, so-called because it applied only to the short period between the Crucifixion and the Second Coming. And this is why it makes such extreme demands on human nature. Later in the history of Christianity, when the Second Coming had receded into the background, these demands were tempered by Greek and Stoic ideas that modified them to a certain extent. But the important point here is that Dostoevsky, after the mock execution, continued to feel this existential core of the Christian ethic with stabbing acuity and made it the basis of his own worldview. This is one reason why, even though he is always dramatizing social dilemmas, he offers answers to them only in terms of personal morality. The strength of his work is that he can show us so powerfully the tragedy of sacrificing the individual and the personal to the abstract or theoretical; its weakness is that he could not integrate the personal and the social in any convincing artistic way. But he is one of the few modern novelists who honestly tried to present absolute Christian values as guides to life. And he does so without evasiveness or compromise, fully aware of all their absurdity and foolishness when seen from the point of view of rational self-interest and common sense.

The mock execution thus marked a turning point in Dostoevsky's life, though all its effects took time to make themselves felt. And his reactions to life in the prison camp, which then followed, were certainly conditioned by its resonances in his sensibility.

Lecture 2

After filling in the background we can now come to the text of *The House of the Dead*. In some ways it is the most unusual work that Dostoevsky ever wrote. It is not a novel, nor is it really a straight autobiography of his prison years. It is what can be called a semiautobiography. By this I mean that everything he writes about, and all the people he describes in the text, actually existed and are those with whom he had contact in the camp. The records of the prison camp still exist, and they fit, more or less, with what he tells us about his fellow prisoners on the factual level, though some details do not completely jibe. For example, the Jewish prisoner, Isai Fomich, is listed in the records as a convert to the Orthodox faith, though there is no indication of this in the book—as a matter of fact, quite the opposite.

Also, Dostoevsky rearranged the chronology of events to give them a greater narrative impact. For example, the reader has the impression that the Christmas celebrations and the theatricals described in chapters 10 and 11 occurred just after the first months of the entry into prison. But, in fact, they only occurred in the

second year of Dostoevsky's imprisonment. The book is thus
carefully arranged and constructed, and we will come back to
that later. But first, we must examine what it tells us about how
Dostoevsky's convictions were changed by this exposure to life
among the Russian peasant convicts. What does he mean when
he speaks of "the regeneration of my convictions"?[5]

We know that Dostoevsky had been involved in a plot to start
a peasant revolution, and we also know that this revolution was
supposed to have been led and controlled by members of the
secret society to which he belonged. The assumption was that
the peasants would follow the leadership of the educated group,
just as in normal social life they carried out their tasks under the
guidance of the upper class.

What Dostoevsky encountered in the prison, though, dis-
abused him of such an idea very rapidly. There he was placed on
a relation of equality with the peasants, or actually on a level of
inferiority, since the constraints under which the peasants were
ordinarily placed in their relation with the upper class no longer
existed. It was here that they could express their real feelings, and
here that Dostoevsky experienced the abyss of class hatred that
actually existed. He describes the difference between how a peasant feels, when he lands in the prison camp, and someone from
the upper classes (part 2, chapter 7). A gentleman, someone from
the upper class, with a Western education, will never be trusted
or regarded as a friend or comrade by the peasants. This is quite
independent of his personal moral qualities and stems entirely
from class difference and the hostile feelings that have developed
over the centuries. In prison, these hostilities were expressed
openly.

5. *Diary of a Writer*, 1873, in F.M. Dostoevsky, *Polnoe sobranie sochinenij* (St. Petersburg, 1895), 9: 342.

In the first letter he wrote to his brother after leaving the prison camp, Dostoevsky said that the peasant convicts would have eaten him and the other upper-class prisoners alive if they had had the chance, so much were they alien and resented. You may, he tells his readers, have had friendly and even fatherly relations with peasants all your lives, but you never really know them. All that is only an "optical illusion" (part 2, chapter 7). The truth only appears when a nobleman is placed in the situation of Dostoevsky himself—when he is forced to become one of the common people.

The consequence of this total alienation between the two groups is very clearly illustrated in "The Grievance" (part 2, chapter 7), which can be read as a comment on Dostoevsky's previous social and political illusions. Here, the peasants had decided to protest against the bad food they were receiving, thus risking the most terrible punishment for doing so. Dostoevsky knew nothing about the plans for the protest because it never occurred to the peasants to tell him, a member of the upper class, about it; he just was not one of them. When he learned what was going on, he wanted to be part of the protest, but he was expelled from the group very forcibly, being led away by the arm, and followed by catcalls and jeers. It's striking to see what he says: "Never before in the prison had I been so insulted" (part 2, chapter 7). We can understand why this particular episode should have struck home so forcibly. He must have suddenly realized to what extent his previous revolutionary ideas had been ridiculously harebrained. And this is no doubt why, in the future, he was convinced that all appeals to revolution in Russia would be doomed to failure. The people would never respond to them. Up until the end of the nineteenth century, he proved to be right.

Such incidents, along with many others in the book, illustrate what Dostoevsky came to feel was the basic problem of Russian society: the yawning split between the classes. How could this be overcome, if at all? There is no direct answer to this problem given in *The House of the Dead*, but one can be inferred from some comments. The book contains a good deal about the punishment of convicts by flogging, and Dostoevsky's impassioned protest against this form of punishment: "Those who have experienced this unlimited power over the flesh, blood, and soul of their fellow-creatures . . . are incapable of resisting their desires and their thirst for sensations. Tyranny is a habit capable of being developed, and at last becomes a disease" (part 2, chapter 3). There were officers who actually enjoyed this task. But Dostoevsky also remarks on the peculiar fact that one officer, Lieutenant Smekalov, was liked by the convicts even though he supervised floggings like all the rest. He was not hated for it because he was only doing his job, while the other officer mentioned, Zherebiatnikov, who really enjoyed these floggings, was loathed and despised. Lieutenant Smekalov was someone whom the convicts "always remembered . . . with pleasure and joy." This ability of an officer to gain the admiration of the convicts intrigued Dostoevsky, since in this individual case it seemed to overcome the estrangement between the classes that was such a crucial problem.

What was there about Lieutenant Smekalov that had produced this effect? It was not because he tried to ingratiate himself with the convicts by pretending to be their equal. This would only have led to the convicts' holding him in contempt for pretending to be what he was not. The reason was—and Dostoevsky underlines the words—because he somehow made them feel that he was one of them. He knew how to speak to the convicts so that on the human level the class difference was both preserved externally and somehow overcome internally. Dostoevsky calls this a special gift, an inborn quality that some upper-class people have so that "they don't seem like white-gloved masters nor exude anything masterly about them; instead, they possess this special common people flavor, inherent to them, and oh, my God, how sensitive the common people are to this flavor!"[6]

What's important here is not so much any external change of social rank or position but the ability to convey a sense of human equality that makes class barriers seem to be irrelevant. This is not really unlike the scene in *Poor Folk*, in which the General shakes Makar Devushkin's hand, and the latter says that this handshake is much more important for him than the money also provided. The reason is that the handshake is a gesture of democratic equality that restores Devushkin's sense of dignity and self-respect as a human being. What Dostoevsky detects in Lieutenant Smekalov can be seen as a broadened plea for the kind of compassion he had already displayed in *Poor Folk*. And this had a very important effect on Dostoevsky's later social-political views and his insistence that the solution to Russia's social-political problems lay not in making any radical changes in its form of government. It was for the upper class to transform their own feelings about the peasants, not to regard them, and especially their religious convictions, as ignorant and obscurantist and backward. Incidentally, many of the crimes described as having been committed by the convicts (not all, to be sure, but the majority) were the result of what the reader of the time might consider a justified revolt against unendurable oppression. Many of the convicts had committed murder, but when Dostoevsky describes the circumstances, we see that, in many instances, the murderer had been provoked beyond endurance by ill treatment.

6. *House of the Dead*, part 2, chapter 2.

One of the striking things in *The House of the Dead* is the role
that religion plays in the book. It turns up everywhere as a controlling force among the peasant convicts, even among the most
hardened criminals. Religion comes to the foreground in the
chapters on Christmas and Easter, when Dostoevsky describes
both the gifts sent to the prison by the townspeople and, more
importantly, the way they were distributed. The convicts stole
from each other incessantly and continually quarreled over what
belonged to whom. But now "everybody was content; there was
not even the slightest suspicion that any alms could be concealed
or divided unequally" (part 1, chapter 10). The very short time
in which peace and harmony prevailed in the camp arose from
this reverence for the holy day, and so Dostoevsky could see that
despite all their crimes the peasants were still capable of sharing
common Christian values of peace and mutual trust. This is also
illustrated by their trust in the Old Believer (part 1, chapter 3)—
to whom they entrusted their money for safekeeping—because
of the piety and sincerity of his faith.

On the surface Dostoevsky couldn't detect in the prisoners
any repentance or remorse for their crimes, but the important
thing was that the convicts still considered their acts to be crimes
in the eyes of God. This is brought out in the account of the
Easter service, when the convicts are taken to church. They all
participated, bought a candle, and then bowed down with a
clanking of chains when the priest read, "Accept me, O Lord,
even as the thief" (part 2, chapter 5). They all thus inwardly accept this designation of themselves as criminals in some sense,
recognizing by doing so the validity of the existing moral law.
So long as this was the case, there was always hope that they
might repent and change their ways. They might have committed crimes, but they hadn't become completely cynical. They

hadn't lost any sense of the difference between right and wrong or tried to justify their crimes as not being crimes at all.

Dostoevsky contrasts them in this respect with the man he hated most in prison, whom Dostoevsky refers to by the first and final letter of his last name, A-v. This was not a peasant but someone with a European education, whose real name was Pavel Aristov (part 1, chapter 5). He had denounced perfectly innocent people to the secret police in return for payment and was finally exposed as a liar and the blackest sort of villain. In prison he had become a spy and an informer on the other convicts for the sadistic camp commander. He was well educated, even good-looking, but totally corrupt and totally cynical, and concerned only with satisfying his "insatiable thirst for the most brutal and beastly bodily pleasures" (part 1, chapter 5). Dostoevsky calls him "a monster, a moral Quasimodo," and writes, " No, fire and death would be better than someone like that in society!"

Such a person is the worst thing for society, far worse than the peasant criminals and murderers. Someone like Aristov[7] has knowingly and deliberately discarded any respect for the moral law, refusing to make any distinction between good and evil and even enjoying his unwillingness to do so. All his education has only encouraged his capacity to wreak evil and harm on others. This contrast between the peasants and the educated Aristov remained with Dostoevsky and became essential in shaping his later point of view. The results of the Western education imported into Russia could be people like Aristov, who weakened the moral standards inculcated by Christianity, in which the peasants still believed. The name of Aristov turns up in the notes that Dostoevsky later made for *Crime and Punishment* and is used

7. Part 1, chapter 5.

initially for the character of Svidrigailov. While his crimes are not the same as those of Aristov, he represents the type of total cynicism that Dostoevsky saw exhibited by Aristov with such enjoyment.

There is another figure in the prison camp memoirs who also affected Dostoevsky very strongly. This was Ilinsky, the prisoner who was supposed to have killed his own father. Dostoevsky used his story later for *The Brothers Karamazov*. This prisoner had been convicted purely on circumstantial evidence, and the impression that this character made on Dostoevsky ("I never noticed any particular cruelty in him") made him doubt that he was guilty: "Needless to say that I did not believe in his crime" (part 1, chapter 1). But the chain of circumstances seemed to be airtight. Later in the book Dostoevsky says that he learned his intuition had been correct—someone else had confessed to the killing of Ilinsky's father (part 2, chapter 7). In *Crime and Punishment*, the character Razumikhin rails against relying on this kind of material, on what seems to be the convincing circumstantial evidence that convicted Ilinsky. He argues that psychological intuition of character should be given more weight. This was what had made Dostoevsky doubt very strongly Ilinsky's guilt in the first place.

There are also other aspects of the book that help the reader understand some other features of Dostoevsky's later views. Although he was a kind of Christian socialist, he had never committed himself to any of the specific socialist utopias because he felt they interfered too much with the freedom of the individual. This already was a theoretical objection before his prison camp years, but his belief in the importance of such freedom was enormously strengthened by what he saw and experienced there.

Over and over again in the book Dostoevsky shows how, under the grip of intense emotions, people will act in what seems to be a totally irrational fashion. Those sentenced to flogging, for example, would sometimes injure or mutilate themselves in order to delay the punishment, though this made little rational sense. The punishment would be given anyway once they had been healed. This is only a small example of the power of emotion over reason that was illustrated in many other features of convict life. The most striking was the relation of the convicts to money, which many of them earned by after-hours labor in the barracks. They used this money to buy vodka, better food, access to women, etc. One would think that they would hoard their earnings very carefully and then spend them in ways that might give them some sensual and material satisfaction.

In fact, they behaved in such a way that to an outside observer their conduct would seem senseless and even demented. They would save their money until they had enough to go on a drinking spree—and would squander it all in this way. In doing so, they would create a disturbance in the barracks, risk terrible punishment, and then be left with nothing. Such behavior was totally irrational, but Dostoevsky understood that it corresponded to a deeper need than what the money could buy. In the first chapter, Dostoevsky explains the psychology of such behavior. What is it that the prisoner ranks higher than money? The answer is: freedom, or at least the illusion of freedom, even if only for a fleeting moment.

When he flings away his money, Dostoevsky explains, the convict has the sense that he is acting of his own free will: he is not obeying orders or bowing to regulations. This need is so great that sometimes, even with model prisoners, it breaks loose, and the convict really seems to have gone mad. Yet maybe all this was caused by "a mournful, spastic desire for an abrupt display of personality, instinctual longing to be his own self, a wish to declare himself and his own reduced personality, appearing suddenly and developing into anger, frenzy, insanity, the eclipse of reason, paroxysm, and convulsion" (part 1, chapter 5). Dostoevsky compares the situation to that of a man buried alive who awakens and tries to break out of his coffin, though he knows it is hopeless. This need of the human character to feel free, to assert its own free will, is thus an ineradicable part of the human personality and perhaps its strongest need.

This emphasis on the necessity for such a feeling of inner freedom became absolutely crucial for Dostoevsky, and we shall see how it placed him in opposition to the radical ideology of the 1860s. But this opposition is no longer only a disagreement about ideas. It goes down much deeper, into the very roots of what Dostoevsky felt he had learned about human life in prison. And we see how all of his experiences come together to emphasize the importance of feeling, emotion, the psyche, the irrational, the satisfaction of inner emotional needs over the logical, the rational, the practical, the utilitarian.

All this had a great effect on Dostoevsky's religious convictions. Although we know very little about his positive religious beliefs in the 1840s, it seems clear that he never became an atheist. He was a Christian of an advanced, progressive kind, who probably downplayed the idea of sin and evil. For him, like Saint-Simon, religion was a kind of social gospel, the application of the morality of Christ to earthly life. The question of Christ's divinity, his supernatural existence, and what that meant for human life had previously not been of very great importance. But as a result of the mock execution, Dostoevsky began to view human life in relation to the supernatural prospect of eternity. And then, certain observations in the camp reinforced this state of eschatological apprehension.

Time and again in the book we see how important it is for the convicts not to give up hope—hope of some even minimal improvement in their lot. Somebody chained to a wall will not give up the hope of reaching the end of his sentence so he can once again walk in the yard, for example. It was hope that kept people alive in the worst and most terrible circumstances. And in one important passage Dostoevsky applies this idea so that it touches on the issue of hope in relation to human life as a whole. And he does so in such a way that it can be read as applying not only to life in this world but to the hope of immortality and eternity in the next.

The passage concerns the forced labor that the convicts performed, and which they found especially burdensome just because it was forced, even though as peasants they had worked harder in freedom. But that, at least, made sense, and they could see they were performing a useful task. But then, in a fashion that is characteristic of the imaginative leaps that he often makes, Dostoevsky invents some sadistic camp commander who sets the convicts a task that makes no sense. For example, carrying heaps of soil from one end of the prison camp to the other and then taking it back. And he writes: "A prisoner . . . would hang himself after a few days, or commit a thousand crimes, so that he would die even, as long as he escapes this kind of degradation, shame and suffering" (part 1, chapter 2). The reason for such a reaction is that, condemned to perform a task that is totally meaningless, the convict would lose all sense that life had some meaning, and thus all hope of any change or improvement (part 2 chapter 7).

This passage is one of the most important in the book. If we transpose it from the prison context of forced labor to that of human life as a whole, it gives us an irreplaceable insight into the roots of Dostoevsky's religiosity. Quite aside from any theological dogma or doctrine, it shows us what might be called the emotional-psychological basis of Dostoevsky's conviction of the human necessity of religion. For him, a life in which there is no God and no eternity meant to be condemned to a life of hopelessness, a life that, in the last analysis, could only lead the human psyche to despair and suicide. This is one of his deepest intuitions, one that shows up again and again in his works. It's not hard to see why Dostoevsky chose hope and faith over reason, and why he often showed in his later novels those who were unable to do so as foundering in madness or committing suicide.

From an artistic point of view, Dostoevsky reordered the actual sequence of events in the prison camp to give them more impact. Though it may seem that the book is just a random series of reminiscences, the events are very subtly organized to communicate to the reader the gradual adaptation of the narrator to the strange and frightening world he encounters. The first six chapters give a panoramic view of prison life that corresponds to someone just looking around to get his bearings in a strange new environment. The focus is not on any one person but on getting a sense of the whole. It is only after this, when the narrator becomes a little more accustomed to this strange world, that he begins to pick out individual people and to focus on them. And then the narrator becomes part of the collective life of the prison and blends in with the others as part of the life they all lead. The structure of the book is thus carefully and unobtrusively arranged to reproduce the internal experience of the narrator; in this way it anticipates some of the more extreme experiments of modern writers to remodel ordinary narrative sequence.

Dostoevsky's narrative technique is usually subjective, emerging from the consciousness of the characters themselves (he is one of the precursors of the stream-of-consciousness novel). But

The House of the Dead is an objective portrayal of the prison camp world. There is very little psychological analysis of the other convicts. Even when they tell their own stories, they stick more or less to events and don't stress their feelings. *The House of the Dead* stands out from everything else Dostoevsky wrote in this respect, and there is much more pure description of scenery and background in it than in anything else he produced. Elsewhere, such descriptions are usually filtered through the feelings of the characters. It's interesting to note that *The House of the Dead* was greatly admired by Tolstoy, who was this kind of objective artist and didn't much care for Dostoevsky's other books.

Just as the narrator (really Dostoevsky, despite the frame story about someone named Goryanchikov, who murdered his wife) tells us little about the inner feelings of the convicts, so he says very little about himself as well. The focus is kept on the others and on the life of the prison camp, not on the narrator's feelings and thoughts—or else they are communicated scenically, as in the narrator's relation to the dog Sharik (part 1, chapter 6) and to the wounded eagle (part 2, chapter 6). The scene with the eagle and the convicts' reaction to it is a fine example of how Dostoevsky conveys the feelings and the longings of the prisoners, indirectly and through a description of the bird held in captivity.

We know that Dostoevsky emerged from the prison camp with a different and much more favorable view of the peasant convicts than he had had at first, but there is no depiction of this transformation. Twenty years later he wrote an article called "The Peasant Marey," a sort of supplement to *The House of the Dead*, and explains how this probably occurred. Why he didn't include it in *The House of the Dead* can only be guessed at; he probably felt it might be too personal for the focus on the others that he wished to maintain.

"The Peasant Marey"[8] helps to clarify what occurred to Dostoevsky, at least as he recalled it many years later, in the prison camp. Whether it should be taken as strictly autobiographical in relation to the prison years or whether he used it to summarize what happened to him over a longer period of time cannot really be decided. What occurred is that at the very height of his revulsion at the loathsome behavior of his fellow convicts, he underwent a kind of conversion experience that was tied up with a memory of his childhood. This experience is linked with the recollection of an incident when he had been treated kindly by one of his father's serfs when as a child he had been terribly frightened. This memory occurred to Dostoevsky during Easter week, when the convicts had more time on their hands and could drink, quarrel, and carouse to their heart's content. He left the barracks to get away from the mayhem, and there met a Polish prisoner, educated like himself, who spoke to him in French and said: "I hate these ruffians." Dostoevsky then went back to the barracks, lay down, and began to think of the past, as he often did, to escape from the sordidness by which he was surrounded. And then he remembered the incident that happened on his father's estate when he thought he had heard someone calling that a wolf was in the vicinity. He ran to a nearby peasant, Marey, one of his father's serfs, who was plowing in the fields.

Marey comforted the little boy by stroking his cheek and blessing him: "All right, all right, make a cross." "But I didn't cross myself; the corners of my mouth were twitching, and that seemed to have struck him the most. He gently reached out to me with his fat finger with its black fingernail, soiled with dirt, and very gently touched my jumpy lips." As Dostoevsky continues, he

---

8. *Diary of a Writer*, January–April 1876, "Muzhik Marey," in F. M. Dostoevsky, *Collected Works* (Moscow: SPb Nauka, 1981), 22: 48–49.

writes, "He was just a male peasant-serf, and I was his master's young son; nobody would find out how he had comforted me, no one would reward him for it. . . . Only God, perhaps, saw from above this profound and enlightened human sentiment . . . that filled the heart of an otherwise coarse, beastly ignorant Russian peasant serf, who was not anticipating or even imagining his freedom then."[9] Dostoevsky then goes on to explain how this memory led to a transformation of his initial feeling of horror at the world of the prison camp. "I walked off, gazing attentively at the faces which I encountered. This vilified peasant, with his hair shaved off, branded on his face, intoxicated, brawling his hoarse, drinking song—he may be the very same Marey; for I can't possibly peer into his heart."

If we take this passage, although written so many years later, as summing up what Dostoevsky felt himself about the effects of his prison years, we can understand why he spoke of these effects as being the regeneration of his convictions. It's not so much that his convictions were changed as that they emerged from a new source. This was the experience of the mock execution, which led him to a deepened conception of Christianity as no longer simply the application of Christ's doctrine of love to the modern world. Christianity had now taken on a deeper meaning for him—its relation to a presumed afterlife—and he had also become convinced that the moral essence of Christianity had really shaped the Russian national character. These were the issues that were to furnish the themes of his major works.

9. Ibid., 22: 49.

CHAPTER 4

Notes from Underground

~~~

Lecture 1

We now come to the analysis of the work that is generally considered to be the beginning of Dostoevsky's great creative period. Up until this time he had been just another author of great talent, with a remarkable gift for portraying pathological states of mind and dramatizing moments of psychological crisis. *House of the Dead* had shown his ability to write in an entirely different, much more objective and descriptive style and had solidly reestablished his reputation for the humanitarianism that had first brought him to fame (although he never again attempted to write anything similar in style to his memoir of his time in prison).

Although after *Poor Folk* Dostoevsky focused on the inner lives of his characters, he invariably used this focus to make a social-psychological point. Sometimes this point became so indirect that it was difficult to make it out, and this is especially the case with *Notes from Underground*. As a result, though it is now generally accepted as a little masterpiece and the prelude to his major novels, it was hardly noticed when it was published. It came out in two issues of a magazine edited by Dostoevsky's brother, a journal that soon vanished from the Russian cultural scene, and no mention of the work was made in any other publications at the time.

The first important reference to it was made only in 1883, and that was by a critic who sympathized with the radicals and called Dostoevsky "a cruel talent," implying that Dostoevsky himself had "tendencies to torture."[1] This sort of attack on Dostoevsky himself was not continued but brought to the foreground what seemed to be his depiction of the attack on the generally accepted moral standards of the time. This was also the time when the influence of Nietzsche, who had called Christianity a "slave morality," became very important. The "underground man" was seen as brilliantly portraying this kind of attack on Dostoevsky's own previous humanitarianism. It came as no surprise that there are those who believed that Dostoevsky himself was on the side of the underground man.

Once critical attention focused on *Notes from Underground*, it began to be seen as one of Dostoevsky's most important works—not as important as his major novels but as their precursor. This is because the psychology of the Underground Man is specifically grounded in a particular ideological context. In *Poor Folk* and *The Double* the reactions of Devushkin and Golyadkin were more or less determined by their place in the social hierarchy of the Russian state. But in *Notes from Underground*, the reactions of the Underground Man stem from specific ideological contexts. And this sets much of the pattern for the main characters of the later novels.

Notes from Underground is a difficult, somewhat obscure, and intricate little masterpiece that is now very famous. The Underground Man has become a symbolic figure of the revolt against reason in modern culture and has been taken to represent either the hideous or the glorious potentialities of the human psyche

1. Nikolai K. Mikhailovsky, *Dostoevsky: A Cruel Talent*, trans. Spencer Cadmus (Ann Arbor, MI: Ardis, 1978).

(depending on the reader's point of view). He symbolizes the ruthless will to strip bare all the conventionalities and hypocrisies of the ego, which is really concerned only with its needs, despite all attempts to conceal this awful truth. In a passage that has become famous, the Underground Man tells the pitiable prostitute Liza, who has come to him for help, "And I say, the hell with the world, as long as I can still have my tea" (part 2, chapter 9). This has been taken as the statement of an ultimate truth about human nature so far as Dostoevsky saw it. It was a statement that delighted Nietzsche, and it was as a result of the Nietzchean influence in late nineteenth-century Russian culture that *Notes from Underground* came to be revalued and interpreted in this sense.

Now, it's perfectly possible to read the work in this way, and lots of famous critics have done so. But one should be aware that in giving this sort of interpretation, we are using the work for our own purposes, in terms of our own contemporary cultural concerns, but not understanding it. In the first place, one may be tempted to assume that the Underground Man is speaking for Dostoevsky and that his words in the quoted statement should be taken at face value. But the Underground Man is a fictional character, and the assumption that he speaks directly for Dostoevsky cannot be taken for granted. It is an elementary critical error to confuse the words of a character with those of the author.

We can also not overlook the situation in which the words were uttered and in what context they were meant to be taken. For example, a reader should consider the scene in which the statement about the tea is made. It is quite clear that the Underground Man is not supposed to be asserting his freedom from the nonsensical moral prejudices that hamper other people, even though he does so in an explosion of rage. Rather, if you take the words in context, he is really expressing his weakness, helpless-ness, and impotence in the face of a situation he is no longer strong enough to control. It is also clear that the prostitute Liza, who is herself capable of genuine love (while the Underground Man seems unable to get beyond his own ego) is meant to be understood as being morally superior to the Underground Man. It is she, if anybody, who represents Dostoevsky's own values, not the Underground Man, even though she is a disgraced prostitute. (We shall see the same pattern later in *Crime and Punishment*.) Shall we simply overlook these facts in interpreting the work and single out only the statement about tea as crucial because we think that to see human nature in terms of a Nietzschean will-to-power is more realistic and relevant?

We can, of course, use the work of the past any way we please. But let us not confuse this use of the work with attempting to understand it in its own historical terms. It is now fashionable to say that, since we can never really know the past on its own terms, we might as well stop trying and consider it in our own. We do this inevitably in any case whether we want to or not. And the question is a very complicated one. My own position is a very simple one. We may not be able to know the past as it really was, but there's no reason we should not make the effort to do so as far as possible. There is no harm in trying, and in doing so, we may be able to avoid egregious historical errors.

Now the first thing to do, if we are to attempt a genuine inter-pretation of *Notes from Underground*, is to make the effort of imagining ourselves back in the world in which it was written. Let us remember Dostoevsky's own historical position. He had been away in Siberia for ten years and returned to pick up the thread of his career in 1860. He wrote a couple of stories just before returning, but his reputation, as we know it, was reestablished by *The House of the Dead*. What is important to understand, as a preface to examining *Notes from Underground*, is what had happened to Dostoevsky in Siberia, and what had been happening ideologically on the home front while he had been away.

First of all, Dostoevsky had become convinced that the real social-political problem in Russia was primarily a moral one. That is, the hatred of the peasants for the gentry could only be overcome by an inner transformation in the attitude of the upper class. Also, the notion of the intelligentsia's ability to lead and control a peasant revolution was simply ludicrous after what he had learned in the prison camp. On a more personal level, his realization of the agonizing need of the human personality to express itself is now linked with the irrational self-destruction of the individual if this need is not satisfied. Finally, if we raise this to a metaphysical level, we all have the need to live in a meaningful world that does not make a mockery of one's self-consciousness and the dignity of one's personality.

All this is important to understand because it helps to explain why Dostoevsky, in the early 1860s, found himself in opposition to the radical intelligentsia. This moment is one of the most important in Russian history, both politically and culturally, and we can only sketch in its background as a means of understanding what occurred to Dostoevsky at this time. Let us begin with the most important historical facts. By the time Dostoevsky came back to St. Petersburg, Tsar Nicholas I had died and been replaced by Alexander II. Tsar Alexander II was no flaming radical, but he was intelligent enough to realize that it was necessary to abolish serfdom. He became known as the Tsar-Liberator, and we should remember that this liberation was the very aim of the revolutionary group to which Dostoevsky had belonged. Thus the tsar had accomplished Dostoevsky's own deepest wish, and from that time on, Dostoevsky became a loyal supporter of the tsarist regime.

Also, Alexander relaxed some of the grip of the police state, liberalized the censorship, and initiated plans to reform the court of law and the army. At first, this created a kind of euphoria in the country, and Dostoevsky returned in the midst of this period of good feeling, when everyone was united behind Alexander II. But new rivalries and tensions soon developed that split the intelligentsia into bitterly hostile factions.

During the ten years that Dostoevsky had been away, a new generation had come on the ideological scene whose leaders were men like Chernyshevsky and N. A. Dobrolyubov.[2] The two had grown up under the influence of the writings of the radicals of the 1840s, such as V. Belinsky, and especially his last phase, when he came under the influence of the atheism and materialism of the Left Hegelians.[3] The intellectual leaders of the generation of the 1860s, as they came to be known, were untouched by the sentimental humanitarianism of early utopian socialism, with its religious overtones. They kept its social-political aims but tried to put them on a new ideological basis that they thought to be more rational. It is a curious fact that many of the Nihilists of the 1860s (as they came to be called) were the sons of priests and had been educated in religious seminaries. But they became

2. Nikolay Gavrilovich Chernyshevsky (1828–1889), an influential Russian philosopher and critic, led the revolutionary democratic movement of the 1860s. Nikolay Alexandrovich Dobrolyubov (1836-1861) was a Russian literary critic, journalist, and poet.

3. Vissarion Belinsky (1811-1848), a Russian literary critic and a critic of the tsarist regime, was an early champion of Nikolai Gogol and Fyodor Dostoevsky. The Young Hegelians, a group of German intellectuals, drew on Hegel's idea that the purpose and promise of history was the total negation of everything conducive to restricting freedom and reason.

bitterly hostile to Christianity once they became converted to atheism under the influence of Ludwig Feuerbach.[4]

However, the philosophy adopted by the new generation could hardly have been more antipathetic to Dostoevsky. It was not only that the Nihilists were atheists and materialists, but they were also determinists, who denied flatly and explicitly that human nature possessed anything that could be called free will. In 1860 Chernyshevsky wrote a famous series of articles called "The Anthropological Principle in Philosophy," which became a kind of manifesto for Russian radicals for at least the next decade. In this work he stated flatly that there was no such thing as free will. Every human action could be explained as the result of the operation of certain scientific laws, and the notion of free will was just an illusion. It's very important to keep this background in mind in reading *Notes from Underground*. Also, Chernyshevsky was influenced by the ideas of English Utilitarian thinkers like Jeremy Bentham and used these as the basis of his own philosophy of ethics.[5]

According to these views, what controlled human behavior was not such an old-fashioned idea as free will but simply the principle of pleasure and pain. Man acted to satisfy his wants and needs according to what was useful for him. People were fundamentally egoists, acting primarily in their own interests and not really thinking of others. But this did not mean that they necessarily had to be evil or selfish. Since their criterion of behavior was usefulness, reason would prove to them that the most

4. Ludwig Andreas von Feuerbach (1804-1872) was a German philosopher and anthropologist.

5. Jeremy Bentham (1748-1832) was a British philosopher, jurist, social reformer, and founder of modern Utilitarianism.

useful thing of all was to collaborate with and to help others. Chernyshevsky called his philosophy rational egoism, and it was based on this absolute faith in the power of human reason to control passion and emotion and just plain selfishness. Dostoevsky, upon returning to St. Petersburg, after what he had seen and felt, and expressed in *The House of the Dead*, could not disagree more.

A few words should be added about the social-political and cultural situation in the early 1860s. The union of the intelligentsia behind Alexander II soon broke up because the radicals believed (and they were right) that, even though the peasants had been freed, they were still saddled with too large a burden of debt: they had to buy their freedom from the landowners. The radicals thus, once again, became hostile to the regime; and it was, in fact, in the early 1860s that considerable underground agitation began in Russia. The earlier generation of the 1840s, by and large, supported the government to a large extent, but not uncritically. For someone like Dostoevsky, whose dream of the liberation of the peasantry had now been realized, the tsar's action was a great moral triumph. And Dostoevsky was afraid, like a good many others, that the rise of underground opposition would only lead to a new crackdown and tightening of government controls.

And this is precisely what happened when revolutionary proclamations began to be distributed throughout St. Petersburg in the early 1860s. Dostoevsky was involved in one incident in 1862. At that time he found one of these proclamations, issued by a group called "Young Russia," which was quite incendiary, attached to the handle of his door. It called for the slaughter of the upper class, including the tsar and his family. Upset by seeing this, he immediately went to pay a call on Chernyshevsky, although he knew him only very slightly. Chernyshevsky was considered as inspiring the radicals, and Dostoevsky asked him to publicly declare his disapproval of such bloody incitations. Chernyshevsky denied to Dostoevsky that he had any connection with them (though this was not literally true), and he later also wrote about this incident, suggesting that Dostoevsky seemed to him hysterical and that he tried to calm him down.[6] What is important here is to see the extent to which Dostoevsky felt himself personally involved and that he tried to intervene. He always saw his public role, both then and in the future, to be that of a reconciler and mediator, not a partisan. And even though he might sympathize with some of the aims of the radicals, he thought that the attempt to realize those aims through outright rebellion could only lead to disaster.

During these years two other works were published that have an immediate bearing on *Notes from Underground*. One is a series of travel sketches, *Winter Notes on Summer Impressions*, which appeared in his magazine *Vremya* (Time) in the winter of 1862–1863 and which were based on his first trip to Europe in the spring and summer of 1862. They form a fascinating document, and it is important to note that the narrator—who is, of course, Dostoevsky himself, but in a highly stylized form—bears a great deal of resemblance to the future narrator of *Notes from Underground*. He is touchy, irritable, worried about his liver, and very argumentative. Even more, the tone, the stance, and even some of the themes of *Notes from Underground* are already present here.

The narrator of these articles is a representative figure, not only of Dostoevsky in person but someone who embodies the complex relation of the educated Russian in general to Europe. On the one hand, Europe contains everything that the Russians have been

6. Joseph Frank added a marginal note: "Whether Chernyshevsky was personally tied up with the group circulating this declaration had never been established."

taught by their education to think good, great, glorious and wonderful. On the other hand, the narrator finds that his own reactions do not correspond to these preconceived ideas. Dostoevsky knows that his readers, educated Russians themselves, have the same preconceived ideas, and so he becomes self-ironical about his own incapacity to measure up to the experience of Europe. But, at the same time, he feels that his own reactions are more genuine and spontaneous than the preconceived ideas he has been taught. And so he makes fun of himself in an ironic tone. But in doing so, he is actually directing his irony at the clichés and hackneyed ideas of those who are also reading his *Winter Notes on Summer Impressions.* The reader is thus implicitly brought into the work and becomes a character inside it, just as will be the case in *Notes from Underground*, where the reader is possibly that man of action whom the Underground Man alludes to as being the opposite of himself. And we find in *Winter Notes* the same kind of double irony that has made *Notes from Underground* so hard to interpret. That is, the narrator is ironical about himself, but he is also being ironic about the reader, who he feels to be judging him at the same time.

The source of this double irony in *Winter Notes* is not only psychological but also social-historical. It arises from this schizophrenia of the educated Russians in relation to European culture, which they both admired and resented. They had been taught to believe, and did believe, that European culture was superior, but at the same time all educated Russians, according to Dostoevsky, were closeted Slavophils. So, the psyche of the educated Russian is split between what it thinks it believes and what it really feels. The *Winter Notes* are important because we see how Dostoevsky makes the connection between his psychology and his ideology that is so crucial for his later novels. The psychological conflicts of his characters have a specific social-cultural significance in relation to a whole conception of Russian history. That is why giving Dostoevsky only a psychological interpretation leads to a crucial misunderstanding.

For the purposes of this lecture, we will focus only on the impressions of London, as described in *Winter Notes*. Dostoevsky roams over that city, and there are some striking pages about the thousands of prostitutes who swarm into the Haymarket district every evening, and particularly on weekends, as well as of the mass drunkenness of the London proletariat who come there at that time. The picture he gives shows Western society, with all its freedoms, in the worst possible light. But of most importance for us here is Dostoevsky's visit to the London World's Fair, which was still in progress when he visited the city. One of its attractions was a building called the Crystal Palace, built entirely of cast-iron, steel, and glass, instead of more old-fashioned materials. This example of modern architecture also housed an exhibition of the latest inventions of science and technology.

Dostoevsky devotes an impassioned paragraph to what he saw there, which filled him with horror.[7] For him, the Crystal Palace became a symbol of the unholy spirit of modernity that had created the moral and spiritual chaos and misery that he saw in London. And this spirit took on the form of the monstrous biblical Beast prophesied in the Apocalypse. For Dostoevsky, it represented the deification and the worship of Baal, the false god of the flesh and of materialism that he saw embodied in Europe, and which the Russians would have to resist. And at the end of the work, writing from France about the plan to establish socialist utopias as a remedy for what he had seen in England,

---

7. Originally published in 1863 in the monthly journal *Epokha (Epoch)*. An English translation appears in *Winter Notes on Summer Impressions*, trans. David Patterson (Evanston, IL: Northestern University Press, 1988), ch. 5.

he rejects such an idea because it would be based on the same principle of materialism.

While Dostoevsky is perfectly willing to admit that there is something very tempting about living on a purely rational basis, and being guaranteed work and social unity, man is an odd creature (*chudak*) and does not wish to live by such calculations. It seems to him that this is prison also (as socialist utopias become equated with prison) and what he really wants is to remain completely free. And he would prefer to be flayed alive and starve, rather than to surrender his freedom to live in such a rationally ordered world, in which he could never feel free to do what he wanted because his interests had been established in advance.

One year later, Chernyshevsky published a novel called *What Is to Be Done?* He was then in prison but was able to get the work past the authorities and the censorship anyway. This book had an extraordinary career, and it became a sort of Bible of the Russian radicals up to and including our own time. It was assigned reading in the classroom during the Soviet period. What is important here, though, is that the same Crystal Palace that Dostoevsky wrote about as the symbol of Baal is used by Chernyshevsky as a symbol of exactly the opposite. It becomes, in a dream vision of the future by the heroine of the book, a symbol of the radiant socialist world that she is imagining for humanity as a whole. The radicals thus took what for Dostoevsky was the symbol of materialism and spiritual death and turned it into their ideal. And in *Notes from Underground*, the *chudak* who had revolted against the socialist utopia earlier (in *Winter Notes*) does so again in a much more complex fashion. Here we have the origins of part one of *Notes from Underground*, and we can now turn to this work and attempt to understand it against this background.

Lecture 2

We have come to the work that marked a turning point in
Dostoevsky's literary career, the point at which he discovered his
mature style. What do we know about its origins?

It began as a kind of review article that he intended to write
on two recent novels for his and his brother's literary magazine,
Epokha. One was by a novelist named Aleksey Pisemsky and the
other was Chernyshevsky's *What Is to Be Done?* How the article
developed into the story is not clear from any of Dostoevsky's
letters, but we can try to see how it might have happened. One
of the outstanding traits of Dostoevsky's journalism is that he
never argues about or expounds ideas in any abstract, impersonal
fashion. His articles are always personal in tone and establish an
intimacy with the reader, as if one person were talking to another.
Dostoevsky was always dramatizing his ideas, sometimes introducing an imaginary opponent who answers what he has to say.
Sometimes this latter voice actually expresses Dostoevsky's own
opinion against the one he is presumably advocating. So it's not
difficult to imagine him beginning an article in this fashion, in-
venting voices as he went along, and then abandoning the article format entirely and turning the story into the kind of dramatic monologue that we have.

This, in any case, is one theory about the way the work came
into being. But we may need to look a little more closely. The first
thing to notice is the commentary to the title. Why was this included, and what on earth does it mean? Most commentators
have thought not very much of it, and in some translations it is
left out entirely. But it is quite crucial and is actually meant to
indicate how the novella should be read. What it tells us is that
the character is fictitious but, even more importantly, that his
traits are the result of the formation of our society. Such people

as the Underground Man, Dostoevsky says, not only exist in Russian society because one can find such bilious and unpleasant types there, but they inevitably must exist in Russian society because of the way this society came into being. The psychological traits of the Underground Man are thus not only those of a private individual but derive from larger social causes—from the whole development of Russian society. To interpret the Underground Man purely in psychological terms thus overlooks what Dostoevsky declares to be his importance as a social-psychological type.

What are the circumstances of the formation of Russian society that produced someone like the Underground Man? For Dostoevsky, the Russian society of his time had been produced, in general, by the influence of European ideas on Russia and, more specifically, by the way these ideas were expressed by the radical intelligentsia of the 1860s. The story had begun as an article about Chernyshevsky's novel, and it was the influence of these ideas on which Dostoevsky focused in part one of the work. Whereas in part two, which takes place twenty years earlier, Dostoevsky goes back to his own past and the ideas he deals with are those of that period. But in both parts, the actions and behavior of the Underground Man, all his passions and emotions, must be seen as influenced and conditioned by the European ideas then prevalent in Russian intelligentsia circles.

How does this work? Now, the first part of *Notes from Underground* can be split into two sections. The first section runs from chapter 1 to chapter 6. Here we get a picture of the Underground Man as a chaos of conflicting impulses, unable to act in any coherent fashion, and even behaving in a way that he recognizes as being senseless and irrational. Over and over again we see him caught in an inner conflict that he cannot resolve, saying one thing at one moment and the very opposite the next moment.

He defines himself as a person who is unable to become anything, neither "spiteful nor good" (part 1, chapter 1) and who
has no character at all. As he says, "A man of the nineteenth
century is indeed morally bound to be predominantly a characterless creature." He also contrasts himself with someone who
has "character, a man of action," but calls this latter an "intellectually circumscribed creature." This man of action is also "a man
of the nineteenth century" but doesn't understand what this
means. This is a preparation for what is to come.

Why is the Underground Man so weak, so "characterless," unable to struggle against all kinds of temptations that he knows
are wrong? He is very self-conscious of the degradation of vice,
but indulges in it all the same. And the more conscious he is of
"the sublime and the beautiful," that is, the very opposite of
vice, "the more deeply [he] would sink into the mire" (part 2,
chapter 1). The very fact that he is so self-conscious makes
him sink into vice even more, and he ends up by enjoying the
very sense of his own degradation. He seems to take a masochistic pleasure in the realization of his own self-abasement, in
his acute awareness of, on the one hand, his knowledge of the
sheer despicability of what he is doing, and, on the other
hand, his unwillingness or inability to behave in any other
fashion. His self-consciousness does not lead to any capacity for
self-control.

As a matter of fact, it leads to the opposite—and this is the
point that Dostoevsky wants to make. For the Underground Man
explains that, in addition to the ordinary consciousness of, say,
the man of action, he has a more developed "intensified" consciousness. "And most importantly and finally—it happens in
accordance with the normal and fundamental laws of intensified
consciousness and inertia, which is a direct consequence of those

laws, and that therefore you not only can not change yourself but you simply can't do anything about it" (part 1, chapter 2). In other words, the Underground Man believes in scientific determinism and is convinced that his will (if there is such a thing) is totally impotent. Here, Dostoevsky is paraphrasing, through the Underground Man, what he takes to be the consequence of Chernyshevsky's denial of the reality of free will. For if there is no such thing as free will, if every human action is simply a predetermined result of the laws of nature, then someone who takes this idea seriously and literally will land in the same dilemma as the Underground Man.

The Underground Man has thus internalized one of the main doctrines of Chernyshevsky. And when he speaks of his intensified consciousness, which differentiates him from the man of action, what he means is that he has become fully aware of what the acceptance of such a doctrine really means. The man of action (that is, the ordinary Russian radical) may accept such an idea, but he does not really understand what he has committed himself to. The Underground Man, on the other hand, embodies what occurs if you really believe in such an idea and imagines what occurs if you try to live by it.

How, for example, can you live in a world in which nobody is morally responsible for anything because you know that there is no such thing as free will and everything happens according to the laws of nature? Dostoevsky tries to imagine such a world, and the example he uses is of somebody being slapped in the face. The person feels insulted and outraged because his dignity as a human being has been violated. But then his reason tells him that it is ridiculous to have such feelings because whoever did the slapping is not responsible for it. The offender was only acting as an instrument of the laws of nature. Or suppose that, after the slap, you feel generous and want to forgive the person who insulted you. But this is equally ridiculous: you can't forgive a law of nature, and the notion of forgiveness implies that you as well as your adversary are both morally responsible (part 1, chapter 2). Since, as a follower of Chernyshevsky, you know this is absurd, what you are left with is the inertia, the inability to do anything, that the Underground Man says is the result of his acute intelligence and self-consciousness. He just remains trapped in this insoluble conflict between his feelings as a human being and what his reason (as represented by the ideas of Chernyshevsky) tells him is the truth.

The problem is that even though the Underground Man is convinced that all this is rationally true, he finds it very hard to live with. He is still a human being with a conscience and with emotions. Even though he knows that if he does something scoundrelly he is not to blame for being a scoundrel (how could he be?), this is yet no consolation because he still feels like a scoundrel. Even though he knows that whoever slapped him is not responsible, "even though it is the law of nature, it still hurts." What Dostoevsky is doing here is to juxtapose the full range of responses of a human being, which includes feelings, emotions, and values, with a belief in reason that simply eliminates them all.

The dilemma of the Underground Man arises because he both accepts Chernyshevsky's idea (and my interpretation was the first one to stress this aspect of the work) and finds that it is humanly impossible to live with at the same time. He refuses to give up his moral conscience (for example, he knows when he is behaving as a scoundrel), while he also knows that he is powerless to act in a morally meaningful way because nobody bears responsibility for their actions. And so, all he can do is to stew over his misdeeds and to conclude that he alone is responsible for everything since there is no one else who can be.

And he takes pleasure in blaming himself for everything, in being a masochist, because this is the only way he has of keeping alive his sense of himself as a morally responsible human being. All his seemingly crazy irrationalism and masochism, which ultimately is a kind of self-punishment, comes from the same source. He punishes himself for not being able to accept the conclusions of his reasoning, which he believes to be true. But he enjoys the punishment precisely because only in this way can he prove to himself that he is still human. This kind of behavior is very similar to the reaction of Dostoevsky's fellow prisoners, who went on drunken orgies to give themselves the sense of being free, even though they very well knew that they were not.

We have here the point of view from which to understand the relation of the Underground Man to the man of action. Who is the latter? The man of action is someone who accepts the same ideas as the Underground Man—a member of the educated intelligentsia, a Russian radical—but who is intellectually too limited to realize what those ideas really imply. He lacks the intensified consciousness of the Underground Man. This is why the Underground Man speaks of the man of action with a mixture of envy and contempt. The Underground Man does envy him because he is able to act; but he is able to act only because he is unaware of what it means to accept the doctrine of scientific determinism.

Moreover, the man of action does not realize that, once he accepts such an idea, all basis of action vanishes because nobody can be held responsible for anything. For example, the man of action wants to change the world for the better in the name of justice. But justice is a moral idea and implies moral responsibility. How can such a notion exist in a world of total determinism? How can anybody's action be considered just or unjust?

So the Underground Man, while he envies the ability of the man of action to act, looks down on him with contempt for his ignorance of what his own ideas really mean. And the man of action repays this contempt with contempt of his own at the Underground Man's inertia, his inability to do anything. But there is an extra twist here that has to be taken into account. The Underground Man is really a mirror image, or a double, of the man of action; he shows what would occur if the man of action were intelligent enough to understand the experiential consequences of his own ideology. The Underground Man parodies the beliefs of the man of action (which are also partly his own) by showing him the moral-psychological consequences that these beliefs would lead to in practice.

Up to chapter 5, the work dramatizes the general impossibility of living in a world from which the ideas of free will (and hence of moral responsibility) have been eliminated. Then, from chapters 7 to 9, we get the social-political application of this same dilemma. What the Underground Man rails against is another idea of Chernyshevsky's—that man acts only according to what is to his own advantage, and therefore that one should construct a society, symbolized by the Crystal Palace, in which all his desires would be satisfied. Chernyshevsky's novel depicts a society in which mankind would not have to struggle to satisfy its desires because they would all have been precalculated and satisfied. And the laws of nature would be so adjusted by reason that it would be unnecessary to will anything because everything would be immediately available to mankind.

Indeed, history shows us that, in the past, man has never acted according to what might be considered his own advantage and has instead spilled rivers of blood. Notice the remark in chapter 7: "Here, take North America—the everlasting union." This was an ironic reference to the Civil War then being fought in the United States. But in the world of the future, man would become some sort of "piano-key or organ stop" (part 1, chapter 7) who would act according to the laws of nature as established by reason and science. But the trouble is that reason and science fail to take into account what for man is the most advantageous advantage of all. And here Dostoevsky uses the terminology of utilitarianism to argue against it: this most advantageous advantage is simply the capacity to exercise one's free will, whatever ridiculous and fantastic consequences it may have. For "reason ... is only reason, and it satisfies only the reasoning ability of man, whereas volition is a manifestation of life as a whole" (part 1, chapter 8). The world of the Crystal Palace eliminates free will and moral responsibility, and the Underground Man rejects it as humanly intolerable, just as he had done earlier with the personal insult.

The argument of the Underground Man is simply that man will never accept a world constructed in such a way as to wipe out his free will. If one is forced to choose between a rational world without free will and a world of chaos in which free will still exists, one will choose chaos. This would seem to suggest that Dostoevsky is on the side of chaos, and he is often interpreted in this fashion, but that is an exaggeration. We should keep in mind that it was not Dostoevsky himself who posed the issue in this way but the radical ideology that he was caricaturing, and his caricature was not a real distortion and was based on the premises of the radicals themselves. It is the radicals who equated reason with scientific determinism and the denial of free will, which Dostoevsky then countered with his defense of irrationalism (the entire human personality) and, if necessary, chaos. Such chaos, however, is brought up only as a possibility, as an imaginary world, a logical projection of the ideas of the radicals.

A frequent mistake is to assume that Dostoevsky, in glorifying chaos as it were, is talking about the world of ordinary experience. But then he adds quite the opposite. After saying that man will go mad rather than be turned into a piano key or an organ stop, he adds: "And after that, how to not fall into temptation, not to rejoice that it hasn't come to that yet and that volition still depends on who the hell knows what" (part 1, chapter 8). In the day-to-day human world, desire is still free.

The next section of the work starts at chapter 10, where we return to the inner emotional dilemma of the Underground Man as we saw it depicted in the first five chapters. For since he accepts all the ideas against which he revolts emotionally, he is being inwardly torn apart by this conflict between mind (in its Chernyshevskyian version) and his moral-emotional consciousness. This is the internal source of the pathos of his mixture of defiance and despair. The Underground Man does not hold up his revolt against reason as a good in itself; on the contrary, he says that he is not against everything considered rational and reasonable but only against the fact that this conception of reason leaves no place for free will. It is only by rejecting reason in this particular form that he can assert his own humanity. What he wants is a world where such a revolt would not be necessary, and as he says, he would lose all desire to stick out his tongue.

This, of course, implies a positive ideal of some future utopia that would acknowledge the existence of free will and moral responsibility instead of eliminating them. And this is the ideal provided by Christ, which Dostoevsky originally intended to indicate in the text more clearly. He complains in a letter to his brother that the allusions to Christ he inserted had been cut out by the censor, and that the meaning had been badly distorted.

This helps to explain various contradictions in this chapter. For instance, the Underground Man speaks of the Crystal

Palace in the first paragraph and says that he is afraid of it because he won't be able to stick out his tongue at it. This is presumably the Crystal Palace in which there is no room for free will. It would be all right if this were a hen coop, serving a useful purpose, but it should not be taken as a symbol of mankind's ultimate ideal. But then he alludes to another Crystal Palace, which he calls "a sham, that its very existence goes against all laws of nature, and that I imagined it out my own stupidity, out of some very old, irrational habits of our generation" (part 1, chapter 10).

But the previous Crystal Palace, as we know, was the embodiment of the laws of nature, and that is why there was no need in it for anything such as free will. How can we explain this inconsistency?

In my view, Dostoevsky, in this chapter, talks about two distinct Crystal Palaces, one of the utopian socialist of Chernyshevsky and the other a Christian one. In the Christian Crystal Palace, one would be free to stick out one's tongue but would choose not to do so, thus exhibiting one's freedom in an act of self-surrender to a higher ideal. So the climax of this part one is the reference to an alternative ideal, but then the Underground Man sinks back into despair because while he can conceive of it, he does not believe in it. And he cannot believe in it because, as a member of the intelligentsia of the 1860s, he does not believe that there is any such thing as free will.

The second part of the work occurs twenty years earlier as the Underground Man begins to remember his past. This takes the reader back to the moral-cultural atmosphere of the 1840s, that is, to Dostoevsky's own beginnings as a writer. This brings up the question of the structure of the work as a whole and the relation between the two parts. Perhaps the best way to consider it is as a diptych, that is, a two-part picture showing two faces and phases of the spiritual history of the Russian intelligentsia. The work goes backward in time, and there is no obvious connection between the parts because Dostoevsky is not interested in the Underground Man as a psychological character. The Underground Man is a representative satirical persona whose psychology only illuminates his ideological convictions or attitudes; it has little or no importance in itself.

The epigraph that precedes the text of part two is taken from a poem by an important Russian poet, Nekrasov, who was a personal friend of Dostoevsky's though the poet was much more sympathetic to the radicals. The cited poem, written in the 1840s, was very famous and was typical of the sentimental-humanitarian ideology of the period from which Dostoevsky's earlier novel *Poor Folk* also came. The fragment of the poem cited describes the confession of a woman who had presumably once been a prostitute and whom the narrator of the poem had rescued from such a life:

> When from the darkness of delusion,
> With passionate persuasive words
> A fallen soul I pulled back up. . . .

The narrator, a member of the intelligentsia, obviously, sees himself as a noble benefactor; and the whole point of this second part, particularly its conclusion with the episode of the prostitute Liza, is meant to reverse this moral evaluation. In the end, Liza is seen as capable of a much more morally genuine and spontaneous love than the young Underground Man.

Part one of the work is a monologue in which the Underground Man broods about himself, but part two is more conventional in that it involves his interactions with other people. Many of these scenes are parodies of episodes in Chernyshevsky's novel *What Is to Be Done?*, which, although written in 1862, reflected the sentimental-humanitarian atmosphere of the 1840s, though they were given a different ideological explanation. To take only one example, an episode in Chernyshevsky's novel depicts one of the heroes, a young doctor, who meets a prostitute, educates her, and lives with her happily until she dies of tuberculosis. This motif is a repetition of the Nekrasov poem, and the episode with the prostitute Liza, in which the beneficent behavior of a member of the intelligentsia is stressed, puts both of these in quite a different light.

In another episode, something that happened in the Chernyshevsky novel is also seen from an entirely different point of view. Chernyshevsky's hero is bumped against in the street without apology by an imposing gentleman of a higher social rank. Instead of taking this affront to his dignity without complaint, the educated commoner turns around, seizes the offender, and rubs his face in the mud. This prideful self-assertion is parodied in the whole comic sequence involving the reaction of the Underground Man to having been bumped in the street. Many other episodes also parody scenes taken from Balzac, Pushkin, and others. The general purpose is to evoke for the reader the social-cultural atmosphere of the 1840s.

What we see here is the Underground Man in his youth as a completely self-absorbed personality. He is so locked in his own egoism—the smugness of his sense of intellectual superiority is so great—that he has lost all possibility of making contact with the real world in some simple, human, common-sense fashion. While the world described in part one was an imaginary projection, in the sense that the behavior of the Underground Man was conditioned by his acceptance of a total determinism, in part two no such doctrine had yet been accepted, and the reader is thus in the world of ordinary social reality and social comedy. It is the Underground Man who is now fantastic, or who lives in a world of fantasy nourished by his egoism. The kind of fantasies that he indulges in are all taken from fashionable European writers.

The action in part two is motivated by the efforts of the Underground Man to establish some sort of normal human relations with others. But this proves impossible because his egoism gets in the way, and he always wishes to dominate others. Not that those he comes into contact with, or the world in which he lives, is seen as any kind of ideal. It is just as stupid and banal as he thinks it is. But this makes his desperate need to obtain recognition from it of his superiority only more ludicrous and grotesque. In some ways, his situation in this respect is comparable to that of Golyadkin from *The Double*, who also wants to be accepted in the world even though he knows this world is totally corrupt.

Because of his need to dominate everyone with whom he comes into contact, the Underground Man invariably arouses antagonism, and he alternates between such attempts and daydreams, nourished by his reading. In part two, chapter 1, he says, "At home I spent most of my time reading." But whenever he emerges from such daydreams, he arouses antagonism and becomes engaged in a contest of wills. Sometimes this is depicted as burlesque comedy, as in the long episode involving his so-called old friends, whom he cordially hates, one and all. Or it is ironic comedy when he sees himself as a glorious benefactor of humanity; but this seeming surge of love for humanity is only another expression of his overweening need to play the leading role. The point here is to show up all the social-humanitarian ideals of the intelligentsia of the 1840s as simply a means of satisfying and flattering their own self-esteem, lacking any real sense of sympathy or understanding of others.

To show up all the shoddiness of this self-exaltation, the story concludes with the episode involving Liza, which turns the Nekrasov poem used as epigraph inside out. Dostoevsky spoke of this episode, in relation to what had gone before, as a shift from chatter to a sudden catastrophe. Comedy quickly thus turns to tragedy when it involves the humiliation and, perhaps, destruction of a suffering soul. It begins with literature (the Underground Man's egoism nourished by his reading) and ends with life (the tragic human consequences resulting from such egoism). What happens is that the Underground Man finally meets Liza, someone who takes him seriously, and who is attracted by his fake sympathy and concern (which is just a more subtle and perverted manner of gaining control over Liza's feelings). He succeeds in breaking down her defenses, which he does on purpose just to toy with her emotions and not because he has any real sympathy with her plight. But he gets carried away by his own success and so, in a grandiose gesture, he invites her to come to him for help.

His remorse when he gets home, his relations with his servant (again recalling *The Double*), his indulgence in daydreams when Liza does not turn up immediately—all this is very funny and satirical. But then Liza arrives, and he realizes to what extent she has been deceived by his words in the brothel. He had presented himself as someone living in a far more luxurious manner than the rather squalid surroundings that she sees. He is humiliated, and his only defense is to insult and humiliate her. But she, unlike all the others, realizing all the suffering that lies concealed behind his insults, refuses to strike back. Instead, now pitying him, she throws herself into his arms in order to console him, and they make love.

This is the human reality of all the exalted idealism that he had imagined in his daydreams but which he is incapable of living up

to in real life. For he is unable to imagine any human relationship except a contest of wills, and so he thinks that by her instinctive gesture of love she has humiliated him. Liza had acted in a
way that he had only pretended to embody. And so, to gain the
upper hand, he must force her back into her role as a prostitute.
That is how the story ends, though she refuses this role by leaving and not taking the money he leaves for her as payment for
her services.

Dostoevsky's story is thus meant as a devastating exposure of
the false idealism of the Westernized intelligentsia, its human
hollowness and sham. And when the Underground Man, at the
end, affirms his superiority to all those who despise him, we
have a repetition of what he said about his relation to the man of
action in part one. Earlier, his intensified consciousness showed
him the human impossibility of living in a world deprived of
moral responsibility. Now we see this same kind of intensified
consciousness revealing the vanity and egoism encouraged by
the Western ideas and values that the young Underground
Man had absorbed from his reading: "I only carried out in my
life to the extreme what you didn't dare to carry out even half-
way ... you mistook your cowardice for common sense"
(part two, chapter 10). Here Dostoevsky is revealing the technique that he used. His method of combating certain ideas
and cultural attitudes is to dramatize and carry out what he
imagined their practical consequences would be if taken
literally.

Notes from Underground had no success when it appeared. It was
hardly noticed at all. One reason was that it was published in
Dostoevsky's own magazine, *Epoch*, which then failed and went
out of circulation. But another reason was that it was so involuted
that it was difficult to interpret, and the point of Dostoevsky's

ideological satire tended to be lost. It was sometimes presumed that the Underground Man was a spokesman for Dostoevsky's own point of view, which is blatantly not the case. Matters became a lot clearer in his next work, *Crime and Punishment*, a more accessible novel. But there, too, we shall see the same relation between a member of the intelligentsia and a prostitute. And it is the prostitute, not the educated character, who expresses the values that Dostoevsky wishes to advocate.

CHAPTER 5

Crime and Punishment

～

Lecture 1

Crime and Punishment is the first work that represents the mature talent of the great Dostoevsky. And it is the first book in which he actually creates the kind of work that is recognized as typical of his mature phase. *Notes from Underground* began this process but more or less as a sport, and Dostoevsky never created anything quite similar to it again, never wrote a work of this ideological complexity as an interior monologue. A few of his later stories, much simpler in content, use the same form, but these stories are minor offshoots of his talent, though wonderful in their own way, and are not in the main line of his artistic development.

This main line runs through his major novels, of which *Crime and Punishment* is the first. The most important thing is that, at the center, there is the same thematic complex already seen in *Notes from Underground*: that is, a character who incarnates one of the ideologies of the radical intelligentsia and who dramatizes its dilemmas. However, now this dramatization is placed in a much broader and more complex novelistic structure. The action is the same in the sense that the ideology is revealed as self-destructive when applied and tested in the actual circumstances of a human situation. But the struggle revealed is now no longer a purely internal one; it is projected into the framework of a much broader image of Russian life and society.

The technical development from *Notes from Underground* to *Crime and Punishment* may seem unexpected at first sight, but it is less surprising if we look at a number of the earlier, minor pieces of writing. Dostoevsky's first works—after he began to publish again and before *House of the Dead*—were two novellas (*The Friend of the Family* and *Uncle's Dream*) portraying larger social milieus. While neither is particularly important for our discussion, both contain much more elaborate dramatic plots than found earlier, and the action is worked out through conceal-ment and surprise. These pieces are quite close to *Crime and Punishment* in technique.

The same is true of another novel that Dostoevsky wrote in 1862 simultaneously with *The House of the Dead*, the novel *The Insulted and the Injured*. This is by no means a successful work, as he acknowledged himself, though the title is often used to characterize the people about whom he wrote, especially during the 1840s. In *The Insulted and the Injured* Dostoevsky is seen imi-tating the French social novel of the 1830s and the 1840s, the kind of work that was called a *roman-feuilleton* because it came out in daily installments in the newspapers.

This kind of novel was developed and raised to the level of art by Honoré de Balzac and Charles Dickens, both of whom Dostoevsky greatly admired, and he worked in the same tradi-tion.[1] Such novels began as popular literature for reading as dis-traction and entertainment, but they had an enormous influence on the development of the novel form. What characterized such works was the use of a mystery or adventure plot and an extremely

---

1. Dostoevsky even translated Balzac's novel *Eugenie Grandet* into Russian.

complicated intrigue with numerous unexpected turns and sur-
prises. An urban setting was also used, either a large city or a small
town. This was not only a background; the urban environment
also was part of the thematic composition of the action, influ-
encing in various ways the feelings and behavior of the characters. The characters themselves are frequently marginal, that is,
living on the edge of society or engaging in activities that place
them outside the social norm. They are usually involved in some
sort of plot action that is never normal and ordinary and that
whips them up to an extreme pitch of tension or excitement.
Their behavior can be considered hysterical, melodramatic, even
unbalanced, and may justify the charge that Dostoevsky's characters are invariably pathological. But this kind of charge simply
refuses to take account of Dostoevsky's thematic aims or realize
that he was writing in a different novelistic tradition than other
Russian novelists of his period.

The Russian critic Leonid Grossman pointed out long ago that
Dostoevsky's writing should be seen in the tradition of the European adventure novel.[2] Such works first developed out of the
English gothic novel of the late eighteenth century, and Dostoevsky indeed wrote about having admired, as a very young boy,
one of the best of these writers, Ann Radcliffe.[3] The gothic novel
was then modernized and urbanized in the early nineteenth
century by such writers as Balzac and Dickens.

This is essentially the world of Dostoevsky's later novels,
which contain certain features of his early works—such as the
Petersburg scene used for symbolic purposes and characters living on the brink of catastrophe because of their social situation.

2. Leonid Grossman, *Dostoevsky: His Life and Work* (New York: Bobbs-Merrill,
1975).

3. Ann Radcliffe (1764–1823), an English author and pioneer of the gothic novel.

But there are no adventure-story plots, with the exception of the ones parodied in *Poor Folk*, and the situations where Dostoevsky brings the characters to the point of collapse are still relatively trivial compared to his later novels. Even though Devushkin and Golyadkin have rebellious thoughts, no murders are committed. But murders do occur in the later novels, and the moral-social dilemma of the characters then takes on a much larger significance. Whereas earlier the characters' problems had arisen because they were in revolt against the rules of their social hierarchy, now they find themselves in revolt, not against the dictates of a particular society, but against those established by their inherited Christian moral conscience.

Grossman also wrote an important article on "Balzac and Dostoevsky" containing a very helpful discussion of *Crime and Punishment*; a good way of getting into the book is to start from some of his observations, particularly on the relations between *Le Père Goriot* and *Crime and Punishment*.[4] Dostoevsky often referred to Balzac's book, which was one of his favorite novels (parodied in *Notes from Underground*), and there is a scene there that is directly related to Raskolnikov. The main character in the French novel, Rastignac, finds that he has the power, through a whole series of circumstances, to inherit a fortune that he badly needs. He has only to agree to have a murder committed by someone else. He asks a friend whether, if the friend knew he could inherit a fortune by killing an old mandarin in China simply by a thought, he would agree to it. Both Alexander the Great and Napoleon are mentioned in this conversation because the friend answers that he is not "a great man" like them and would not take on such a responsibility. This exchange raises the same sort of ultimate

4. Leonid Grossman, *Balzac and Dostoevsky* (Ann Arbor, MI: Ardis, 1973).

question that is central to *Crime and Punishment*. Is it permissible for "a great man" to agree to the commission of a murder?

Other obvious connections are shared by Balzac's novel and *Crime and Punishment*. There is a structural similarity in the letter that Raskolnikov receives from his mother, which reveals the poverty of his family and the desperate plight of his sister. This letter has the purpose of giving an additional altruistic motive to his crime. Exactly the same thing happens in Balzac's novel, where a letter about Rastignac's sisters (he has two) also provides an altruistic motif to his behavior (he doesn't commit a murder, but he does exploit others to advance himself). His personal will to power—what can be called the Napoleonic motif, which also appears in *Crime and Punishment*—thus acquires a moral dimension that gives it more complexity since it is no longer purely personal and self-centered. This is the major thematic difference between *Crime and Punishment* and the novels of Stendhal and Balzac, which also link the Napoleonic image with the theme of a personal will-to-power. The altruistic motif is much more accentuated in Dostoevsky and given a universal moral-religious significance. In Balzac, it still has only a personal character. Rastignac wants to help his sisters, but Raskolnikov, though he wants to help his family, views their problems only as part of his larger ambition to help humanity.

This relation to Balzac is only one of the many currents flowing through the novel. Dostoevsky read very widely and can be related to many other European writers, but the most important influences come from his own Russian tradition. A reader understands that Dostoevsky himself presents Raskolnikov's ideas as being quite commonplace and not at all out of the ordinary. For instance, there is the very important tavern scene, during which Raskolnikov overhears a conversation, the topic of which, by coincidence, is his own idea of killing the old pawnbroker for the good of humanity (part 1, chapter 6). The discussion of his idea between a student and a young officer occurs over tea and after a game of billiards. Dostoevsky places this conversation in such an ordinary setting because he wants to show that it was the kind of idea that was in the air at the time. It was not something that Raskolnikov had concocted himself because he was some kind of pathological personality. And the narrator stresses this point by commenting: "Of course, this was an example of the most ordinary and commonplace youthful talk and ideas that he had heard more than once before, in different forms and on different subjects" (part 1, chapter 6). In other words, such ideas were those that educated young Russians were talking about and pondering all the time.

Indeed, it can be verified that the ideology of Russian radicalism in the early 1860s, as Dostoevsky portrayed it in his novel, was an odd combination of English utilitarianism, French utopian socialism, and a doctrine of mechanical materialism. This had already been attacked by Dostoevsky in *Notes from Underground*. But at the same time, there was another current of radical thought that had some slight differences with the first. These differences did not concern politics as such, since there was no real politics of any kind in Russia in any case, but it was expressed in literary and social-cultural terms by various groups. One such group consisted of followers of Chernyshevsky. The second did not differ with these ideas essentially, but its members were younger, more radical in temperament, and ready to carry these ideas to greater extremes than Chernyshevsky himself had done.

The leading advocate and ideologue of this younger group was Dmitry Pisarev, a young aristocrat of good education and a fiery temperament—whose essays are still a pleasure to read. He is famous in Russian culture for having written a series of articles attacking Pushkin, in which he carried utilitarianism to the extreme of declaring that art was a waste of time in view of all the social problems that the country had to deal with. Since the most pressing problem was that of poverty, everyone should devote themselves to working to alleviate it and not waste their time with art. He also urged, in one of his articles, that the younger generation should destroy everything (or try to) on the theory that only what resisted such destruction was worthy of enduring.

These two factions of the Russian intelligentsia came to a head-on clash in 1862 with the publication of I. S. Turgenev's novel, *Fathers and Sons*. Turgenev's hero, Bazarov, is often taken as a glorification of the radical intelligentsia of the early 1860s, but he was not considered as such by the followers of Chernyshevsky, who attacked the book very harshly on the ground that it was really a slander on the intelligentsia, not a true image of them at all. They objected to Bazarov's feelings of superiority, his haughtiness toward others, his contempt for everyone but himself. True, he despises the upper class, believes in science and utilitarian values, and wants to help the people. He is also a plebeian himself, not a member of the landed gentry, and refuses to behave according to upper-class manners. But he never displays any sentimental attachment to the people and is a supreme individualist. He is more of a plain, ordinary egoist than a "rational egoist," whose reasoning would persuade him that his own interest is best served by helping others.

There was, in particular, one scene in the book that shocked the older radicals. This occurs when Bazarov is walking in the village and passes the hut of a well-to-do peasant. He is in the company of his friend, the young liberal landowner Arkady, who says hopefully that in time all peasants will be able to live as well as that. But Bazarov comments bitterly that, by then, weeds will be growing out of his grave. In other words, he is unable to subordinate his own personal fate, the certainty of his own death, to the utopian dream world of the future that Arkady evokes.

However, Pisarev wrote a famous article in which he praised Turgenev for having truly depicted the new radical, and he accepted as accurate and praiseworthy all those features of Bazarov that the other radicals had rejected or simply overlooked. His individualism, his arrogance, his nihilism (Bazarov calls himself a nihilist)—all this is praised and taken as typical of the new radical who was supposed to be evolving out of the old. To show how great and heroic Bazarov was and how much superior to the ordinary conventions of social life, Pisarev says that Bazarov would commit a murder if he felt like doing so. If he doesn't, it's not because of any objection to such a crime but because it just doesn't happen to appeal to his taste. He would be perfectly capable of stealing and robbing if this suited his convenience at any particular time.

Pisarev's article on Turgenev's character Bazarov was only the beginning of the controversy between these two radical factions. All historians of Russian culture agree that the group who may be called the real nihilists won the argument in the intervening years that led up to *Crime and Punishment*. And their victory was aided by certain external factors. One was the Polish uprising against Russian rule in 1863. This was supported by the majority of the Russian radical intelligentsia, but in the population as a whole, it led to a patriotic enthusiasm for putting down the rebellion (a patriotism in which Dostoevsky shared). More importantly, it changed the image of the Russian people, which the radicals previously regarded as a potentially progressive and revolutionary force. That kind of anti-Polish patriotism had a very disillusioning effect on the young radicals, whose opinion of the people thus underwent a sharp change.

This change already had been foreshadowed in Pisarev's article and reinforced its effect. For Bazarov is not only glorified as a superior individual who exists above the law; he is also contrasted with the vast mass of unthinking, unconscious ordinary mortals who merely submit and accept their fate. This mass, Pisarev wrote, does not make discoveries in science or commit crimes. This relation between great intellectual achievements and crime is precisely the same as we'll find in Raskolnikov's article. And it is on behalf of this mass, Pisarev writes, that the other group think and suffer, seek and find, fight and go astray—other people who are eternally alien to the mass, who even look on it with contempt, yet at the same time never cease working on its behalf so as to improve the amenities of its life. This is the very admixture of traits that Raskolnikov will represent four years later: the character who both looks down on the vast unthinking mass with contempt yet destroys himself because he wishes to become their benefactor.

Little or no attention has been paid to the relation between the genesis of *Crime and Punishment* and Pisarev's article, or the whole movement of Russian culture in which Pisarev played so important a role. Critics have sought far and wide for the source of Raskolnikov's ideas, and the most diverse influences have been suggested, from Balzac's novels to Hegel's theory of "the great man" to Pushkin's Hermann in *The Queen of Spades.*[5] The characters of both Balzac and Pushkin may well have entered into

5. Joseph Frank added in the margin of his lecture notes: "Leonid Grossman thought that he had found them in Balzac's novels, where the master criminal Vautrin enunciates a doctrine of the will-to-power. Philip Rahv has pointed to Hegel's theory of 'the great man' in his *Philosophy of History*, someone like Napoleon who accomplishes a great historical task and should not be judged by ordinary moral standards. Other sources have also been mentioned, for example, the character of Hermann in Pushkin's *Queen of Spades*. He also thinks of himself as a limited Napoleon and com-

Dostoevsky's conception and helped to shape it, but these characters all lack the altruistic aspect, and they are certainly not the source of Raskolnikov's character, with his inner conflict between an egocentrism that believes itself capable of transcending all moral-social boundaries and a deeply and emotionally genuine love for other fellow human beings, or at least with a capacity to respond to them on that level whenever he is moved to do so.

Whatever the source of Raskolnikov's ideas, Dostoevsky was trying to show how the assimilation of certain advanced Western ideas into the ideology of the radical intelligentsia could lead to the dilemma dramatized by Raskolnikov. Pisarev, for example, was a supporter of the capitalizing and industrializing of Russia at all costs because he believed it would advance the general enlightenment. This is all part of the influence of English utilitarianism among the Russians that started with Chernyshevsky. And it explains why Dostoevsky could make the parallel he draws, and quite accurately, between the ideas of the petty sadistic tyrant Luzhin and that of Raskolnikov himself (part 2, chapter 5). Both base themselves on utilitarian reasoning. For Luzhin, by looking after your personal interest, presumably you also help others. For Raskolnikov, you have a right to kill one person to help a much greater number. If you start with the ideas of Luzhin, and really carry them out consistently, you can end up with those of Raskolnikov; in neither case are you concerned with old-fashioned moral ideas. The difference is that, while Luzhin pretends to be interested in the welfare of others, he is obviously an arrant hypocrite as well as a petty sadist. Poor Raskolnikov genuinely wants to help others, and this is why he finally breaks down.

---

mits a crime, but his motive is the desire to gain a fortune. The altruistic motif is missing in all of them."

There are also other characteristics to be brought up, such as the growing influence of social Darwinism in Russia and the general acceptance of such theories. Social Darwinism served then and later, not only in Russia but in the West as a whole, as a scientific justification of oppression. The most successful had shown themselves to be the fittest and strongest in the course of evolution and thus had the right to rule over the weaker who had also survived. As one of the origins of racism, this was generally accepted as the last word of science in the nineteenth century. An illustration of the use of social Darwinism in the text is the passage in which Raskolnikov observes a lecherous gentleman pursuing a young woman in the street, who is drunk and looks as if she has already been violated. Raskolnikov feels sorry for her, begins to intervene, but then changes his mind after the following reasoning: "A certain percentage, they say, must be used up every year . . . used up . . . and to hell with it, I suppose; to refresh others and get out of the way" (part 1, chapter 4). Since a percentage of this kind has to sink into prostitution for the welfare of society, there's no point in interfering with this law of nature, and the reader sees the sudden reversal of Raskolnikov's feelings.

It's interesting to note that Dostoevsky's magazine, in an article on the French translation of Darwin's *On the Origin of Species*, was among the first in Russia to point out the inhuman moral implications of using Darwinism, based on observing natural and animal phenomena, as a theory of society. And it was also Dostoevsky's journal that carried on a continual polemic with others. One of his articles, centering on the split between the two radical factions, was called "*Raskol* among the Nihilists" (*raskol* is the Russian word for "split" or "schism"), and the name of Raskolnikov probably derives from this source. In addition, several years earlier, Dostoevsky wrote a letter to Turgenev about

Fathers and Sons, telling him how much he admired the book; Turgenev answered, in a letter we do have, that Dostoevsky was one of the two people who really understood the book. So we see how steeped was Dostoevsky in this novel and its main figure, Bazarov. And so Raskolnikov is Dostoevsky's version of Bazarov, what Pisarev thought Turgenev's Bazarov represented.

Lecture 2

In the last lecture we touched upon the idea of the ideological background, so important for a proper understanding of *Crime and Punishment*. This doesn't mean that the work is about these issues in any strict sense. Dostoevsky is not writing a social-political novel in which people argue about or simply illustrate the various ideas of the 1860s, though there are dialogues in which he does parody such ideas. He does so with a character like Lebezyatnikov and some of the speeches of Razumikhin. But what made Dostoevsky so great a writer is precisely that he did not stay on the level of the ordinary arguments of his time but used them rather as the source of his inspiration. He began with them—but then thought these ideas through to their ultimate consequences in moral-psychological terms. And it was on this imaginary level that he was able to dramatize them—always starting from something that existed in the social-cultural arguments and polemics of the time.

One of the criticisms that has sometimes been made against my approach to his works is that in focusing as much as I do on the social-cultural context, I reduce his novels to being a reflection of the limited issues and questions of his own day. What is the universal importance and relevance of such novels as *Crime and Punishment* if one always has to be searching out ideas and ideological quarrels that have long been forgotten?

There is something to be said for this point of view. Too often a concentration on the context, whether it is historically social-cultural, as in this case, or whether it comes from other sources, such as gender and race for example, tends to lose sight and forget that if we are studying a great writer, we are doing so precisely because he/she was able to raise this context onto a higher or more general level. A great work of art always transcends the conditions of its creation and has meanings that go far beyond what its own period might have thought about it.

In that sense I would agree with such critics, but I don't accept that my own work is guilty of this critical fallacy. Or at least, being aware of it, I do my best to avoid falling into such an error. At the same time, I do try to avoid another error that, so far as Dostoevsky is concerned, is much more widespread. This is to interpret him exclusively in terms of the most general psychological and philosophical categories, without attempting to investigate what these actually meant in his own time. One could easily say, for example, and without being wrong, that the real theme of *Crime and Punishment* is the eternal conflict in Western culture between love and justice, and one could analyze the work in terms of such general moral ideas. But this is not the place to start from because what's not really known is what these words actually mean within the context of the time and country in which the novel was created and in relation to the characters in which such ideas are embodied. And unless it becomes clarified, we are apt to be quite wrong in understanding the meaning they had for Dostoevsky. Hence, one has to start from the ground up, as it were, if one is to reach the heights by the road that Dostoevsky as author meant for us to follow.

In mid-1860s Russia, the ideology of radicalism took on a strong streak of individual glorification. Bazarov, as the ideal figure of the younger radicals, became a kind of Nietzschean superman, beyond good and evil, though this comparison should not be taken too literally. For Bazarov, as Pisarev saw him—and this image actually became more important than the way he is shown in the book itself—combines a love-hate relation to mankind with a desire to be its benefactor and savior. What Dostoevsky wished to do was to show the impossibility of combining these two attitudes in real life, just as he had done in Notes from Underground.

There he had portrayed the Underground Man as psychically torn apart by his commitment to a set of rational ideas that are in direct conflict with his emotions as a human being. Here Dostoevsky does the same thing, except that the controlling ideas now lead to the experiment with a murder, one that his conscience, as a moral personality, cannot support. One aim of the book is to depict the moral-psychological chaos caused by this internal conflict. Another is to indicate that true altruism or love of mankind can only be rooted in the Christian ethos of self-sacrifice, not in a rational utilitarian idea of social justice that allows for murder in the name of a larger social good.

At one time it was believed that Dostoevsky was not much of an artist, and this opinion went hand in hand with the view that he was really a kind of inspired genius who had no more control over his works than over his own life. And such a perspective about him was greatly encouraged by the widespread influence of the Freud article,[6] which tended to identify his personality with all the vices of the characters he portrayed. Ever since the publication of Dostoevsky's notebooks, which only began to appear in Russia in the 1920s, it became quite clear that he was a highly self-conscious writer, who thought long and hard about

6. Sigmund Freud's essay "Dostoevsky and Parricide" was published in 1928 as part of a German collection of scholarly articles on The Brothers Karamazov.

the construction and organization of his works. He continually complained about the fact that he always had to write for periodicals and under pressure of deadlines (because he needed the money) and could not afford to polish his works like Turgenev and Tolstoy.

As a matter of fact, far from lacking in artistry, it is now recognized that he was ahead of his own time in the narrative techniques he employed. He actually anticipated important developments of the modern novel, such as the fusion of narrator and character (called free indirect discourse), his presentation of character subjectively, and his original manipulation of time sequence. All three of these innovations are used in the structure of *Crime and Punishment*.

A number of commentaries have been written on the question of Dostoevsky's artistry as a novelist. And Mochulsky, for example, an excellent critic, calls the present book "a tragedy in five acts with a prologue and an epilogue."[7] Although it is quite possible to read the book as containing such a structure, this perspective is insufficient and misses certain aspects that, I think, are important. For me, a more important structure is provided by the manner in which the action is constructed so as to reveal Raskolnikov to himself, to allow him to solve the mystery contained in his own character. The book really depicts the coming-to-consciousness of its protagonist, Raskolnikov, about the truth of his own behavior, the real meaning of what he has done compared to the initial meaning that he thought his actions would have. This is why Raskolnikov offers so many explanations for his crime as the book goes along, and critics have spoken of the indeterminacy of his motivation and the problematic nature

---

7. Konstantin Mochulsky, *Dostoevsky: His Life and Work*, trans. Michael M. Minihan (Princeton, NJ: Princeton University Press, 1971).

of the modern personality. Whatever one may think of the modern personality, Dostoevsky was concerned with that of Raskolnikov and knew exactly what he was doing.

There are three motivations presented in the book. The first is in the tavern scene and can be called a utilitarian-humanitarian motivation. The second motivation is the Napoleonic motive displayed in Raskolnikov's conversation with the investigator Porfiry Petrovich. The second one is often considered the very opposite of the first, but it actually repeats the same idea as the first one, only on a more historically elevated level. The third motivation is heard in his confession to Sonya, and here he declares that he wanted to kill solely to discover whether he was merely a trembling creature or a louse, or whether he had the right to step over the moral law. And he specifically eliminates any utilitarian motive either for himself personally or a future benefactor of mankind.

The passage from one motive to the other is the gradual revelation of his real motive, or rather the realization that his initial humanitarian aim, no matter how deeply felt, was really a self-deception; or rather, that the means chosen to accomplish it could only be put into practice if the third motive took over and completely dominated the personality. At the root of the utilitarian humanitarianism of the radicals one finds total egoism. This is the same point made satirically in *Notes from Underground* by the parodies of the dreams of the benefactor mode.

Part one of the book is constructed in a very skillful fashion that is generally overlooked. It is also important as evidence of Dostoevsky's great skill in the use of a technique such as the flashback and in the manipulation of time sequence. Essentially, part one is composed of two sequences. One begins with the visit to the pawnbroker and moves forward in time to the completion of the crime. This sequence, externally, is composed of the trial visit to the pawnbroker, the encounter and conversation with Marmeladov, then the encounter with the drunken girl on the boulevard. Interspersed with these episodes is a series of flashbacks that move backward in time and evoke the past. There is indeed the letter from his mother, then his childhood recollection of the beating of the horse, then the conversation in the tavern in which he hears the humanitarian-crime theory he has been brooding over discussed by the officer and the student.

This is the first statement of Raskolnikov's motivation, which has both a "rational" component that is utilitarian and an emotive-altruistic one that may be called Christian (since the aim of helping suffering humanity derives from the Judeo-Christian component of Western culture). Murder is rational and justified if the amount of good flowing from it outweighs the amount of pain and suffering it may have caused. The problem is that, in order to commit a murder, one has to overcome all the key emotional and moral forces in the personality that moved the murderer in the first place to come to the aid of humanity. There is an internal contradiction here that will be played out in the account of Raskolnikov's fate.

A number of critics have pointed out an inconsistency between this first motivation and the second, Napoleonic one, but they may have simply overlooked Dostoevsky's own anticipation of the passage from the one to the other. In the conversation between the officer and the student, the officer objects that no one would kill the old pawnbroker, even though she deserved to die, because "that's nature." And the student answers that nature has to be corrected and guided, "otherwise you couldn't have a great man." Obviously, from the very start it required "a great man" to carry out even the utilitarian-altruistic crime. This theory, in its two faces, is fully revealed to the reader just before the crime is committed, though this involves a complete inversion of the time sequence. The actual sequence of events, not as it is given in the book, is such that the tavern conversation occurs at the beginning of the events leading to the crime. A careful reader will notice that, chronologically, this overheard conversation occurs before Raskolnikov is introduced to us in the opening pages; Raskolnikov is already brooding about it at the very beginning of the novel. But in the book the tavern conversation and the crime occur within only a few pages of each other.

Why does Dostoevsky arrange the order of events in this way? The answer, it seems, is because he wants the reader to recall the tavern conversation and also the summary of the process of Raskolnikov's reasoning given in the next few pages. Raskolnikov's own moral casuistry had convinced him that, unlike ordinary criminals, he would not be emotionally upset or disturbed by the crime. But the reader observes quite the opposite. It is not a calm and cool Raskolnikov who acts but someone in a frenzy of hysteria, who behaves as if he were in a kind of hypnotic trance. In this way Dostoevsky undercuts the theory of the crime and forces the reader to pose the question: what is the real reason for committing this crime, since the ones given by Raskolnikov to himself are false?

The answer is implicitly given in the two interweaving sequences previously mentioned. For they show, in the first place, the good Raskolnikov, who cannot endure the suffering of his family and hates the cruelty and injustice that he sees around him everywhere. It is the good Raskolnikov who leaves money at the Marmeladovs' out of pity and spontaneously goes to the aid of the girl who has been abused. This is the irrational, unreflective, instinctive Raskolnikov who loves humanity, wishes to relieve its suffering, and thinks he will achieve that good by committing this crime.

But each time, this innate altruistic core of his personality becomes twisted and distorted by utilitarian calculus or some

other so-called "scientific" reasoning. And when he becomes involved with such a pattern of thought, it ends up by turning him
humanly into the very opposite. We see this when he leaves the
Marmeladov house and cynically thinks that they don't need his
few coins since they are living off Sonya (part 1, chapter 2). The
same thing occurs with the girl on the street, who is just a
percentage and thus no longer a human individual. When
Raskolnikov begins to reason with such ideas, he becomes a
cold-hearted monster who really hates and despises mankind
instead of feeling any sympathy for it. But at this stage of the
book Raskolnikov is not yet aware of the split between what he
thinks he is doing and what is happening to his character under
the influence of these rational ideas. Clearly, Dostoevsky intended to make the reader aware of this split; or, at least, he
shows it in action all through part one of the novel. And so, he
has prepared the reader for much of the action that follows,
including the famous article and his final confession to Sonya.

The manner in which ideas operate on the personality is shown
not only in the case of Raskolnikov but in several other scenes
of this first section. Early in the novel, in the tavern scene,
Marmeladov tells Raskolnikov a humiliating incident: how he
asked for a loan although he knew beforehand that his request
would be refused. And he even asks why anyone would want to
give him a loan since he can't repay? Out of pity and compassion?
But he also knows that "compassion nowadays is even prohibited
by science" (part 1, chapter 2)—that is, political economy, a
science based exclusively on utilitarian reasoning, not on sen-
timents of any kind.

Dostoevsky counterpoints these two situations through one
very significant detail in the scene on the staircase, when Raskolnikov meets the police official who had come to inquire about

the accident with Marmeladov later in the novel. The official observes that Raskolnikov "is soaked with blood" (part 2, chapter 7), referring to the bloodstains from carrying Marmeladov's body. And Raskolnikov responds in a peculiar way that he is all covered in blood—and then smiles. The bloodstains on his clothes from the murder had filled him with terror, but the bloodstains from his charitable deed fill him with exhilaration and new hope. This is only one example of how careful a writer Dostoevsky is in making every detail count.

At this point in the book, Raskolnikov has dissociated his original theory into two separate components, and the altruism and the egoism no longer have any organic relation to each other. The altruism flows into the Marmeladovs and involves his relation to Sonya; the egoism now stands alone and supports his struggle against the investigating attorney who suspects him, Porfiry Petrovich. This is why the reader learns, shortly after this dissociation becomes clear, about the article entitled "On Crime" that Raskolnikov had previously written. While his egoism has been displayed earlier in action, now the reader is given its full reach and force as a worldview that had barely been hinted at before. It is important to remember that Raskolnikov's article was written even before the conversation in the tavern and his first visit to the pawnbroker. It is thus the original source of the crime, even if only from a purely temporal point of view. And it is brought forward now and developed (the article had only suggested the idea that Raskolnikov now expounds) at the point where Dostoevsky wishes to foreshadow the final confession (part 3, chapter 6).

The meeting with Luzhin destroys Raskolnikov's first motive for the utilitarian-altruistic crime. The second, Napoleonic motivation, still has an altruistic component, even though the great man aspect rather puts it in the shade. But this combination is destroyed in the great pages of inner monologue after Raskolnikov is accosted by someone in the street and called a "murderer" (part 3, chapter 6). It is then that he realizes the impossibility of being both a great man and a benefactor of mankind. The great men are not made like that: they kill ruthlessly to attain their own ends, and they could not care less about how many lives they destroy. Raskolnikov's own theory has thus betrayed him into accomplishing a deed he had not the psychic strength to support; he was not really a great man because he could not completely eliminate his moral conscience as they had done. And Dostoevsky has him trying to kill the wretched old pawnbroker in his haunting dream, but he is unable to succeed.

It is only when Raskolnikov's original theory has split apart in this way that Sonya and Svidrigailov come to the foreground to carry the story forward. Both are mentioned earlier, but are not as important until the point where they both serve as quasi doubles to Raskolnikov. Both present him with one or another extreme consequence of his initial doctrine. His altruistic component is deepened into Sonya's all-encompassing Christian love, one carried to the utmost limits of self-sacrifice. Sonya comes from a long line of prostitutes in the French social novel of the 1830s (you can easily find one of her prototypes in Hugo's *Les Misérables*, one of the longest-running shows on Broadway). Dostoevsky's use of such a character, a prostitute who becomes a spokesperson for the highest Christian values (the theme he continues from *Notes from Underground*), is exactly the sort of thing that Nabokov ridicules. It also led to objections from the editor of the journal in which the novel was serialized, and Dostoevsky had to rewrite the chapter in which Raskolnikov and Sonya read together the Gospel of St. John about the raising of Lazarus (part 4, chapter 4).

Even though Sonya can be considered a hackneyed character, Dostoevsky manages to raise her to a level of intensity and
purity that is unrivaled. The reason is that he is able to present
the idea of self-sacrifice with such uncompromising force.
Dostoevsky is willing to make this idea totally irrational, in the
original Christian sense, with no regard for anything except the
immediate effect of the act to ameliorate human suffering. It is
as if time itself did not exist —or is totally overlooked. What is
important is to respond completely to human suffering at every
instant. This is the interim ethics, which many theologians believe is the soul of primitive Christianity. Dostoevsky expresses
it in one little episode in part 4, chapter 4—the only time that
Sonya admits to being ashamed of anything. It's not prostitution
she is ashamed of, because that is her self-sacrifice for others. It's
that she refused to give poor, dying Katerina Ivanovna some or-
namental cuffs she wanted. "What use are they to you?" she
asked her. Sonya is, of course, right from every sensible point of
view. But, as Pascal said, the heart has reasons that reason alone
cannot comprehend.[8] These are the reasons that Sonya is constantly opposing to Raskolnikov's arguments, which are never
refuted as such but which, so to speak, refute themselves. For in
back of them looms the horror of the murders, and we see them
through the lens of Raskolnikov's tortured spirit. Sonya has no
arguments to answer Raskolnikov, but her self-sacrificing faith
gives her a spiritual strength, whereas he is plunged into torment
and moral turmoil.

The scenes between Raskolnikov and Sonya are justly famous
for their power, but some of the subtleties of their interchange
should not be overlooked. One of these is Raskolnikov's attempt

8. Blaise Pascal (1623–1662), French physicist, philosopher, and mathematician,
in his book *Pensées*.

to persuade Sonya that the two of them are alike since both have transgressed the moral law. Raskolnikov thus tries to identify himself with Sonya and, as it were, mitigate his own sense of guilt and failure. But in so doing, he (or Dostoevsky) only brings out the enormous difference between the two more effectively. He says to Sonya, "You laid hands on yourself, you destroyed a life ... your own (that makes no difference)" (part 4, chapter 4). This last phrase is marvelous because it obliterates all the difference between Christian self-sacrifice and a sacrifice that others make for the benefit of mankind. The latter is based on a rational ethic of utility; the first on a spontaneous and unselfish response to human suffering.

By the time Raskolnikov confesses to Sonya, he has become aware that his intoxication with power is incompatible with love. Great men like Napoleon, as already said, do not worry about the people they destroy because the greatness of their aim (or so they think) overrides all other considerations. But this has not been the case with Raskolnikov, who now realizes that in the crime he was only testing himself. He was trying to prove that he was a "great man," and assess whether or not he could overcome the morality that was holding him back against all the conclusions of his reason. He had to break through the restraints of his conscience, shaped by Christian values, and he now realizes that he has failed.

It is often said that the confession scene does not give one clear reason for Raskolnikov's action, but this seems to me a misreading. He goes through all the rationalizations that had previously concealed the egoistic roots of his behavior from himself but then breaks through to the final recognition. It is when he shows himself deliberately cultivating his own difficulties, exacerbating his hatred both of himself and for mankind, and finally turning that hatred into an act of supreme defiance, that we see the forces working in him all along. And when he finally declares that might makes right ("the man who dares much is right in their eyes"), Dostoevsky intervenes as narrator to mark the difference between this and the other explanations: "Sonya understood that this gloomy creed had become his faith and his law." Sonya's consciousness, we know, is always that of the author.

All the same, even though Raskolnikov is now aware of the true nature of the impulses that had led to the murders, he cannot persuade himself rationally that he was wrong. He knows that he cannot endure the emotional burden of the crime, but at the same time no rational argument can convince him that he was wrong in his justification of the great man. His failure was that of an individual, of himself, not of his theory. He continues to think that the greatness of a great man derives from his total indifference to any concern for others. Dostoevsky resolves the problem of converting Raskolnikov to a different point of view in two ways—one individual, the other more general.

Svidrigailov is used to reveal to Raskolnikov the full implications, in private, personal life, of the great-man theory, which recognizes no power higher than the satisfaction of all one's desires, the sexual and sensual included. Svidrigailov can be considered a Luzhin carried to a higher power, who refuses to mask his desires under a veil of hypocrisy. He is Raskolnikov's intellectual equal, and his subplot with Dunya parallels that of Raskolnikov with Sonya. But he goes to death while Raskolnikov goes to a new life. Porfiry Petrovich, the magistrate, is also Raskolnikov's intellectual equal, and I wish I had more time to spend on him. One can perhaps imagine Porfiry as the mature Dostoevsky speaking to a new, young incarnation of himself once again in the grip of illusory subversive ideas. This would help to explain the melancholy that Raskolnikov notices on his face during their third interview.

Returning to Svidrigailov, we recognize a remarkable character, who again lifts a stock figure—the lecherous, upper-class villain who preys on women—into a powerful, death-haunted symbol of a life empty of all (or almost all) spiritual substance. From his very first appearance we see how Svidrigailov can only conceive of life, and even of life after death, in repulsive, degrading, and disgusting forms. And the last important event before his suicide is the dream of the little girl he has rescued—the symbol of innocence—turning into a whore. It is because Svidrigailov cannot break out of the circle of horror caused by his own self-indulgences that he commits suicide. Dostoevsky uses him also to solve some of the practical problems in the text, and this might raise some questions. But he manages to make it convincing because of a suppressed longing for goodness, an ironic desire to escape from himself and his role, that makes his behavior verisimilar.

The final resolution occurs in the epilogue, which has aroused a great deal of critical objections. But it seems to me, the role of the final dream is decisive. There is no rational argument against Raskolnikov's "great man" theory, but there is a visionary one emerging from his subconscious. The dream universalizes the "great man" theory so that it infects everybody; the result is a world of the war of all against all, the state of nature as described by Hobbes, whose man is a wolf to man. This is a world in which reason has destroyed all irrational moral-emotional ties between human beings. And it is the chaos resulting from this destruction that finally converts him to the religion that is the source of those emotions that caused him to confess.

CHAPTER 6

The Idiot

~

Lecture 1

Dostoevsky's most important work after *Crime and Punishment* was *The Idiot*. In some ways this is the most mysterious and baffling of all Dostoevsky's novels. But it is also the one that has a special appeal to a large number of readers. In one of his letters, Dostoevsky wrote, "All those who have told me it is my best work share something special in their mentality that I always found impressive and pleasing."[1] One of the reasons for this is probably that *The Idiot* is the most autobiographical of all his novels, in the sense that one can see how he used elements of his own life to portray the main character, Prince Myshkin.[2]

But Dostoevsky always transformed such personal events in his work to give them a larger meaning in relation to the problems of his own time (as in *Crime and Punishment* or *The Devils*) or in relation to the larger issue of religious faith that concerned him during the post-Siberian period of his life. And certainly in modern literature *The Idiot* stands out as one of the greatest works in which an attempt is made to project a contemporary image of a Christ-figure.

1. F. M. Dostoevskii, *Polnoe sobranie sochinenii v tridtsati tomakh*, ed. V. G. Bazanov et al. (Leningrad: Nauka, 1986), vol. 29, book 2: 139, February 14, 1877.

2. At the root of the last name "Myshkin" is the word "mouse" (*mysh'*), hence the ironic (if not oxymoronic) combination of the princely title and mousy last name.

One of the principal events Dostoevsky uses from his own life is his mock execution just before being sentenced as a political conspirator in 1849. This experience marked the beginning of his transformation from a writer who projected a world mainly on the social-political and moral-psychological plane to one whose horizons broadened out to the religious and the metaphysical. It is this experience of man's confrontation with death that turned him into the writer he later became, an experience that he tries to embody in *The Idiot*. The writer and the protagonist both suffer from the same disease: epilepsy. It is striking that while this disease presumably gives Prince Myshkin access to a momentary experience of plenitude and world harmony, the disease is also seen as being incompatible with the ordinary demands of earthly human life.

At first sight it may seem very difficult to handle this novel within the terms of our previous approach. Essentially, the framework has been to see *Notes from Underground* and *Crime and Punishment* as artistic polemics aimed at the ideas of the radical intelligentsia: the doctrines of Chernyshevsky were explored in *Notes from Underground*, while in *Crime and Punishment* the target became the image of the new radical as it appeared in Turgenev and was developed by Pisarev. In effect, Dostoevsky explores all the moral and human consequences of such ideas and of such an image. And he traces the problems back, just as he did in *Crime and Punishment*, to their ultimate roots in a psychology conditioned by the religious heritage of the Russian Orthodox tradition. It might seem, however, that the same schema can hardly be used for *The Idiot*.

It is true that Dostoevsky does include a sequence involving the Young Nihilists (in part 2, chapter 8), where he satirizes to some extent these young radicals. But he also gives them some redeeming features all the same, and he makes them ridiculous and pathetic rather than in any way dangerous or sinister. The crime in the book is committed by Rogozhin, a merchant's son troubled by doubt but still steeped in the Russian religious tradition and not someone motivated by emotions arising out of radical ideas or as a consequence of radical ideology. Rogozhin's crime is a crime of passion, not of ideas. So in this sense the pattern used by Dostoevsky in his earlier works breaks down.

All the same, the previous general framework can still be applied, if broadened to interpret the events that occur in the book. This framework is based on attempting to accommodate some general absolute value or ideal to the real world of human passion and human feeling and revealing its limitations in this way. In *Crime and Punishment* Raskolnikov's theory of a humanitarian crime fails because to carry out a crime requires the release of an egoism that then becomes an end in itself.

The same strategy is also at work in *The Idiot*. But what makes the book so remarkable is that the ideal and absolute value that Dostoevsky is testing here happens to be his own. For, if Dostoevsky here creates a character who embodies the highest ideals of Christ (as he conceives them), then he also shows the incompatibility of these ideals with a life as lived in the world. These ideals do not bring about any change that in any way improves human life. On the contrary, as was pointed out long ago, Prince Myshkin and his "curse of saintliness" (a curse, rather than a blessing) make things more complicated for everybody, ultimately leading to Prince Myshkin's breakdown and return to Switzerland. His ideal goal is defeated, just as was the case with Raskolnikov. And so what remains is the underlying pattern of the clash between the real and the ideal.

This similarity has been generally overlooked or attributed to a weakness or failing of Dostoevsky's artistic capacities. It has also been said that Dostoevsky wanted to write a book showing

Christianity to be triumphant and competent to solve the moral and ethical problems of this world. And some evidence for this can be found in his notes for *The Idiot*. Throughout the novel Prince Myshkin continues to hope that this will be the case. For example, he believes that he can help solve the love-hate relationship between Rogozhin and Nastasya. But, of course, this outcome never occurs; quite the opposite: Dostoevsky's own Christian ideal goes down to defeat against his will and against (presumably) his artistic intention.

Did Dostoevsky actually mean to write a novel in which his Christ-figure appeared as a kind of miracle worker who brought people happiness in this world? This is suggested by the story of Marie in part one (chapter 6), which tends to set up a pattern of possible resolutions that one expects to be carried through. But it is difficult to imagine that Dostoevsky thought he could keep the whole novel in this sentimental and edifying tone—or that Prince Myshkin could solve the problems of the other characters in the same way. In the inset parable it should perhaps be noted that it is on children that Prince Myshkin acts, and that children, due to their innocence, do not differentiate between the kind of love with which Prince Myshkin loves Marie and the love that their parents may feel for each other. Myshkin's love for Marie stems from pity and compassion; the love between their parents is sexual and passionate. Dostoevsky was well aware of this thematic issue; one of his notes reads: "*THREE* KINDS OF LOVE IN THE NOVEL:

(1) passionate and impulsive love—Rogozhin.

(2) Love out of vanity—Ganya.

(3) Christian love—the Prince."[3]

---

3. F. M. Dostoevskii, *Polnoe sobranie sochinenii v tridtsati tomakh*, ed. V. G. Bazanov et al. (Leningrad: Nauka, 1974), 9: 220.

The material in Dostoevsky's notebooks is so varied and diversified that it is difficult to draw any conclusions from it. What it makes clear, in any case, is that the external history of the book is one of the most complicated in the whole Dostoevsky corpus. There is one passage in his letter of January 1868 that is of great importance in illuminating his own ideas. Written just after Dostoevsky had sent off the first five chapters of part one of *The Idiot*, it attempts to explain what he had been trying to do, namely, to write a novel about "a positively beautiful human being."[4] This statement is quoted very often, but the rest of the letter is even more important for understanding the novel.

"There is only one positively beautiful character in the world—Christ," he writes, "so that the appearance of this boundlessly, infinitely beautiful person is, of course, an infinite miracle in itself (the Gospel of St. John is about this; the whole miracle is in the incarnation alone, the manifestation of the beautiful)."[5] Then Dostoevsky turns to Don Quixote and Pickwick and Jean Valjean (in *Les Misérables*) as representing a related effort to create Christ figures; but he finds them all inadequate.[6] For Dostoevsky, Don Quixote is ridiculous as well as beautiful. And what makes him ridiculous is that Don Quixote tries to act in the world to realize his ideal. Then Dostoevsky seems aware that to give Prince Myshkin more than a passive role would make him equally ridiculous. The same is true for Pickwick, who is lumped

4. F. M. Dostoevskii, *Polnoe sobranie sochinenii v tridtsati tomakh*, ed. V. G. Bazanov et al. (Leningrad: Nauka, 1985), 28: 251.

5. Dostoevsky's letter to his niece, S. A. Ivanova, January 1 (13), 1868. F. M. Dostoevskii, *Polnoe sobranie sochinenii v tridtsati tomakh*, ed. V. G. Bazanov et al. (Leningrad: Nauka, 1985), 28: 251.

6. *The Posthumous Papers of the Pickwick Club* by Charles Dickens was published in serialized form from 1836 to 1837 and in book form in 1837.

together with Don Quixote. As for Jean Valjean, a convict who
escapes and then becomes a benefactor of humanity, he awakens sympathy because he is a victim of social injustice and suffers for this reason.

But Dostoevsky rejects such literary models. "I don't have
anything of that kind [in my work]," Dostoevsky says. "Absolutely nothing."[7] Prince Myshkin is made to inherit a fortune
soon after the book opens and is thus cut off from this source
of appeal. He is neither actor nor victim but a presence, a kind
of moral illumination, which is how Dostoevsky had envi-
sioned Christ in the Gospel of St. John. The miracle is not in
anything that Myshkin does but in the mere fact of his presence as a spiritual force. It is what this spiritual force does to
other people that precipitates the action of the book. It is most
unlikely that Dostoevsky ever intended to write a book in
which his Christ figure would play an active leading and guid-
ing role in resolving conflicts; rather someone who would
leave an indelible trace wherever and with whomever he came
in contact.[8]

The critics who assume that Dostoevsky was defeated in some
sense by his own creation—that is, unable to portray his Christian ideals in viable realistic terms—assume a conception of
Christianity that was not at all Dostoevsky's own; namely, the
notion of religion as some sort of social gospel—active and
successful in the world—was not the view at all of the mature

7. "I don't have anything of that kind [in my work—MB.], nothing at all, and for
that reason I am terribly afraid of it being a positive failure." F. M. Dostoevskii, *Polnoe
sobranie sochinenii v tridtsati tomakh*, ed. V. G. Bazanov et al. (Leningrad: Nauka,
1985), 28: 251.
8. Part 3, chapter 1.

Dostoevsky; his notion of religion did not imply that at all. But while he may have come close to something like this kind of Christian socialism in the 1840s, it no longer corresponded to what he believed when he wrote *The Idiot*. By this time his Christianity had become that of the humiliated and suffering Christ, come to be sacrificed in this world to bring about its redemption and salvation but in no way to become its sovereign.

One of the greatest recent students of Russian Christianity, G. P. Fedotov, wrote a classic book in two volumes, *The Russian Religious Mind*, in which he defined the indigenous Russian religious tradition as being essentially kenotic, as it stresses Christ's surrender of his divine nature (he is, after all, the God-man) when he descends to earth.[9] He appears not in resplendent majesty but as a suffering human being who does not resist evil and is a sacrificial victim. Dostoevsky felt this aspect of the Russian religious tradition very profoundly and eventually gave it one of its greatest expressions in the "Legend of the Grand Inquisitor" (in *The Brothers Karamazov*, book 5, chapter 5).

This Russian kenoticism helps explain some particularities of *The Idiot*—for example, in Prince Myshkin's relationship with Aglaia Epanchina, who wants him to learn how to fight a duel, since she is sure he will be challenged after the incident in the park at Pavlovsk. Aglaia assumes that Prince Myshkin will behave according to the code of honor of the time, which has nothing Christian about it at all, indeed quite the opposite. She identifies Prince Myshkin with Pushkin's heroic "Poor Knight," a Roman Catholic warrior of the European Middle Ages, though

9. G. P. Fedotov, *The Russian Religious Mind* (Cambridge, MA: Harvard University Press, 1966).

Myshkin is actually quite the opposite of any such type.[10] According to the ideas of the Slavophils shared by Dostoevsky on this point, the combination of religion and worldly power embodied a Roman Catholic ideal. And at the end of the novel, Dostoevsky marries Aglaia off to a supposedly heroic Polish Roman Catholic count, presumably wealthy but actually without a cent, and she eventually falls into the clutches of the Roman Catholic Church.

This provides a general framework for an approach to the religious conceptions of the book. But there is another document that must be taken into account here, and it offers the only direct glimpse into Dostoevsky's actual religious beliefs. It is also of the greatest importance in understanding the character of Prince Myshkin. This document is a notebook entry that Dostoevsky made while keeping a nighttime vigil beside the coffin of his dead first wife. The date is April 16, 1864—that is, while he was working on the second part of *Notes from Underground*—but its words really lie at the heart of his conception of Prince Myshkin. It is the only firsthand nonfictional source that tells us what Dostoevsky thought about some of the essential doctrines of the Christian faith. Dostoevsky was trying to define his convictions for himself, and he wrote the entry under conditions that allow its reader to accept it as a valid expression of his deepest beliefs.[11] It is curious that this notebook entry has never attracted much attention until quite recently, even though it was translated and

---

10. A. S. Pushkin's poem "Poor Knight," written in 1829, describes a knight who, after seeing a vision of the Virgin Mary, devotes his life to the Church and to defeating the infidels. Afterward, when he is dying, the Virgin Mary protects him from the devil, who wants to take him to hell.

11. F. M. Dostoevskii, *Polnoe sobranie sochinenii v tridtsati tomakh*, ed. V. G. Bazanov et al. (Leningrad: Nauka, 1980), 20:172.

published in German in 1926 and printed in Russian in Europe in 1932.

The entry begins: "Masha is lying on the table. Will I see Masha again?" The question posed immediately thus is that of immortality. Dostoevsky's question may seem to indicate some skepticism; it is not an affirmation of faith. But neither is there any rejection of the possibility. The question most likely refers to the form in which existence after death continues rather than to the fact of such existence itself. This is the sense also of the passage in *The Idiot*, in which Prince Myshkin speculates about the feelings of the man awaiting execution and which reproduces some of the details of Dostoevsky's own impressions following his mock execution.

He looks agonizingly at the sunlight reflected from a church steeple, which can be viewed as a detail or imbued with a symbolic meaning: "It seemed to him that those rays were his new nature and that in those three minutes he would somehow melt into them. . . . The uncertainty and aversion for that new thing which would be and was about to come were awful" (book 1, chapter 5). The feeling here is that of a terror before the unknown, a terror that would have no reason for being if Dostoevsky had been convinced that some sort of consciousness, in a form that he could not imagine, would cease to exist. As a matter of fact, Dostoevsky had said himself that, after the execution, he "would be with Christ."

The notebook entry, which also takes up the question of immortality, begins with some moral reflections. "To love another as *one's self*," he writes, "according to the commandment of Christ, is impossible." This statement is rather extraordinary. But this does not mean that Dostoevsky thinks the commandment of Christ to be misguided, for he explains that it sets forth an ideal toward which all humanity is striving and which Christ himself incarnated in His life on earth: "Christ alone was able to do this [love others as himself], but Christ was an eternal ideal toward which a person strives and should strive by the laws of nature." This peculiar appeal to the laws of nature may remind a reader quite unexpectedly of Chernyshevsky. But the laws of nature referred to here are not the latest scientific discovery but the laws of man's spiritual nature revealed to him by Christ, whom Dostoevsky calls "the idea of man incarnate." It was these very laws of nature, taken over by the radical intelligentsia, that Dostoevsky opposed.

Why is the commandment of Christ impossible to fulfill on earth? Because "the law of individuality on earth binds. The *I* [ego] obstructs," answers Dostoevsky.[12] Thus the sheer fact of human individuality itself, quite apart from any other aspect of human character, is the great stumbling block to the fulfillment of the law of Christian love. But, in spite of this, Dostoevsky says that it is now "as clear as day," since the Incarnation, that the highest, final development of the individual, is to imitate Christ and sacrifice his individuality: "The highest use which one can make of his individuality, of the full development of the ego, is to seemingly annihilate that ego, to give it wholly to each and everyone whole-heartedly and selflessly. And this is the greatest happiness." Dostoevsky claims this merging of "the ego and the all" "the law of humanism," and "the paradise of Christ." All history, according to him, whether of humanity as a whole or of each man separately, is "only the struggle and striving to attain this goal."

Present here is the connection between Dostoevsky's apocalyptic view of history and the inner moral-spiritual crises and dilemmas of his characters. Both were part of the same struggle

---

12. F. M. Dostoevskii, *Polnoe sobranie sochinenii v tridtsati tomakh*, ed. V. G. Bazanov et al. (Leningrad: Nauka, 1980), 20:172.

to realize what the great American theologian Reinhold Niebuhr in his book *The Nature and Destiny of Man* called the "impossible possibility" of fulfilling the law of Christ.[13] While Niebuhr was not referring to Dostoevsky, his ideas help to clarify Dostoevsky's Christian point of view.

This struggle is continually necessary, and Dostoevsky believes that it can never be fully accomplished on earth. His reasoning is that, if this is the final goal of humanity, then its accomplishment, in fact, would be the end of human life and history. It would no longer be necessary to live, since human life has been defined as the struggle to reach this ideal. Hence, in Dostoevsky's words, "[a person] on earth is only a developing creature, consequently, not a finished one but transitional."[14] And so, the very highest development in any individual of the capacity to realize the law of love remains necessarily incomplete. This is very important in trying to understand Dostoevsky's depiction of Prince Myshkin. Even the very highest embodiment of the Christian ideal on earth (from Dostoevsky's point of view) has to be seen as failing to achieve the ideal.

Dostoevsky then uses this conclusion as an argument in favor of immortality. If life on earth is necessarily incomplete, then there must be "a future, heavenly life."[15] But his text remains obscure on this future life and how it is related to what we know as life in this world: "What it will be, where, on what planet, in what center, whether in the final center, i.e., in the bosom of the universal synthesis, i.e., God?—we do not know." The only thing

13. Reinhold Niebuhr, *The Nature and Destiny of Man*, 2 vols. [1941–43] (Louisville, KY: Westminster John Knox Press, 1996).

14. F. M. Dostoevskii, *Polnoe sobranie sochinenii v tridtsati tomakh*, ed. V. G. Bazanov et al. (Leningrad: Nauka, 1980), 20: 173.

15. Ibid.

we do know about it though is what has been foretold by Christ— and he cites the Gospel of Matthew: "They neither marry nor are given in marriage, but are like angels in heaven" (Mark 12:25 and Matthew 22:30). Thus the one ideal condition of future heavenly life that Dostoevsky recognizes is a total sexlessness.

And as he develops this point, he returns to the problem of egoism and individuality that he had raised earlier. He attacks marriage and the family almost in the same way as the radicals, but, of course, with a totally different aim in mind. The radicals were in favor of more freedom for women, and the traditional concept of the family stood in their way. For Dostoevsky, the family was also an obstacle, but he saw it as a breeding ground for egoistic self-centeredness: "Marriage and the giving in marriage," he wrote, "is as it were the greatest departure from humanism, a complete isolation of the pair from everyone (little is left for *all*). The family—that is the law of nature [JF: in the usual sense of reproduction], but still abnormal, egotistical in the full sense . . . The family is the most sacred thing on earth for a person, for by means of this law of nature man attains the development (that is, generational change) of the goal. But at the same time, also according to the laws of nature, in the name of the final ideal of his goal [JF: man's spiritual nature], one must continuously deny it. (Duality)."

Arguing with the atheists and speculating about immortality and its mystery, Dostoevsky, in a few sentences, sums up the inner conflict of all individuals on earth: "Mankind strives towards an ideal opposed to his nature. When a man has not fulfilled the law of striving towards the ideal, that is, has not through love sacrificed himself to people or to another person (Masha and I), he suffers and calls this state a sin. And so, man must unceasingly experience a suffering which is compensated by the heavenly joy of fulfilling the Law, that is, by sacrifice."

These words have the closest connection with *The Idiot*. It is important to note that an author holding such beliefs could scarcely have depicted a human analogue to Christ, or even Christ himself, as capable of resolving human moral-social conflicts. Since the law of Christ is fundamentally opposed to the very basis of human individuality, its effect can only be to precipitate an inner struggle in anyone who takes it seriously. This is exactly the effect it has on Myshkin himself and on all the people with whom he comes into contact. By stirring their conscience, he leads them into a conflict with their usual selves.

This notebook entry also helps a reader to understand why Prince Myshkin himself, even if he is not torn between egoism in the narrower sense and the Christian law of love, is still caught in the same conflict on a higher level because human love itself, sexual love, the basis of the foundation of the family, is itself egoistic for Dostoevsky. Myshkin's love for Aglaia is of this kind, necessary for the perpetuation of life, but still egoistic. And this love comes into conflict with his love for Nastasya Filipovna, which—similar to his love for Marie—is based on pity and compassion. Hence, Myshkin's conflict can be expressed in terms of the distinction made in modern theology between two kinds of love, which have been called *eros* (sexual love) and *agape* (Christian love).

Agape and Eros is the title of a great work of theology by Anders Nygren, and it is essentially a study of the impact of Christian ethical ideas on the world of classical antiquity, which was governed essentially by Greek ideas.[16] The Greek idea of love was defined by Plato. It begins with the love of beauty, sensuous

16. Anders Nygren (1890–1978), a Swedish Lutheran theologian, published his two-volume *Agape and Eros* in 1930 and 1936.

beauty, and leads to a desire for the possession of the loved object. It can, of course, stay on this level, but in finer spirits it also stimulates the desire for the possession of the highest good, which, for Plato, lies in the contemplation of "the Ideas" (his term for the equivalent of what is considered to be God in monotheistic religions). It leads out of the world of sensuous, earthly experience and into that of a mystical contemplation of the Absolute.

The important point is that this kind of love is ultimately egoistic and selfish. It starts with the desire for possession and continues to remain oriented by this goal, even if it turns away from physical possession and becomes refined and spiritualized. Also, it is always linked with the idea of the worth and value of whatever is being loved—the love is a function of the value of the loved object. Christianity, according to Nygren, introduced a new and opposite idea of love into the world. Mankind did not have to aspire upward, as it were, to obtain the object of the highest good. God himself came down to man, in the person of Jesus Christ, offering what was the highest value as a free gift. But mankind was not really worthy of this gift, and therefore the relation between value and love is reversed. An *eros*-love aspires toward the highest value, but an *agape*-love goes from higher to lower. The Christian God loves sinners (all of mankind sinned in the Fall), and therefore the entire scale of Greek classical values is reversed. In primitive Christianity, it is not the worthy who are loved but the unworthy—or, at least, this is one possible extreme consequence of Christian ethics. And the highest form of love is embodied in the self-sacrifice of Christ, who is the paradigm held up to all of mankind as an eternal aspiration.

Nygren is a cultural historian and theologian not a literary scholar, a Lutheran, and not Russian Orthodox, but his ideas are helpful in trying to understand Dostoevsky. For example,

Marmeladov's speech in the tavern in *Crime and Punishment* is a striking statement of the paradox that God prefers the unworthy and will save them because they are aware of the depths of their debasement. And Prince Myshkin's normal humanity, his love for Aglaia as a possible future wife, interferes with his *agape*-love for Nastasya Filipovna, whom he pities and wishes to help. Ultimately, this is the conflict within himself that Dostoevsky shows Prince Myshkin as unable to resolve.

Dostoevsky does not really believe that a perfect *agape*-love is possible for a human being. It is accessible only to Christ. Humans, by the very nature of their being, will always retain a component of *eros*-love. But—by the same token—since the advent of Christ, it is toward the *agape* ideal that mankind should strive.

Lecture 2

The Idiot is the most difficult of all Dostoevsky's works to analyze, partly for extrinsic and partly for intrinsic reasons. It is, at the same time, perhaps the most fascinating and uneven of his great works, as well as the most intimate of all his books. Dostoevsky himself said that he was always happy to receive letters from readers who admired the novel, those kindred souls who understood him or at least sympathized with him. Perhaps, he felt this way because he gave so much of himself so directly in this novel.

The first thing to keep in mind is that this book has a history different from all the others. Beginning with *Crime and Punishment* they were all written from scenarios whose main outlines had been established in advance, with only details that had to be filled in as Dostoevsky went along. This all changed when he decided to write *The Idiot*. Actually, the character who became

Prince Myshkin was initially imagined in a totally different form. Dostoevsky claimed, after sending off the first installment, that he had decided to take a chance, just as at roulette, and see what turned out. It is safe to say that this is the only time that he really won!

Some of the uncertainty in the handling of the book springs from his abrupt decision to write a novel about "a perfectly good [or absolutely beautiful] human being" just about a month before he was required to turn in the first installment. Dostoevsky had the character before his eyes, or in his imagination, but he had no clear notion of the narrative action in which he would be engaged.

The analysis begins with a simple question: what is the theme of the book? The answer can be stated with equal simplicity: it is the Passion of Christ—but with a difference. Prince Myshkin is a Christ-like figure, who appears in the world, is destroyed, and, in a certain way, leads to the destruction of others while inspiring them at the same time. But this comparison is really too broad to be of much help. For Myshkin is a man, not a supernatural being. He is a man trying to incarnate, or somehow inspired to incarnate, the pattern of Christ; but he is unable to do so because he is not a disembodied spirit. In a certain sense, he is ultimately betrayed by his humanity.

Prince Myshkin, as a character, comes out of the theological ideas discussed in the previous lecture. It should be recalled that Dostoevsky believed that to fulfill the commandments of Christ on earth would be impossible because the ego would stand in the way. Even the family, the purest and most moral earthly love, is an expression of the ego and prevents the fusion of individuals into a loving earthly unity. There is a fundamental contradiction between Christ's commandment of universal love and sexual love of any kind, not because sexual love is impure in any conventional sense but because it is necessarily egoistic. Only at the end of time, when man will be transformed into some kind of asexual, seraphic being can genuine universal love be possible.

Prince Myshkin, plausibly, represents the highest incarnation of this ideal accessible to mankind in its present form. But he is torn apart by the conflict between his still-human and quasi-divine natures. Christ is a God-man who, presumably, can combine the two, but it is his appearance on earth that was a miracle. Prince Myshkin cannot resolve the conflict between his individual love as a man and his desire to follow Christ's commandment of universal (Christian) love.

This conflict can only be resolved at the end of time; and one of the specific aspects of Myshkin is that he lives *in* time, but as if time had no continuity or duration. He is haunted by the eschatological apprehension of the end of time, just as Dostoevsky himself was, which is why he is so obsessed with the experience of death. In part one of the book, what motivates Prince Myshkin is this acute sensitivity to death as manifested in his three accounts of the subject.

The first one occurs in the conversation with the doorman who refuses to let him in to the Epanchins because of his strange appearance in foreign clothes. But when the prince describes to him the suffering of a man waiting to be guillotined, the social barrier is broken down, the doorman's suspicion entirely vanishes, and he allows the prince in. Later, there is the conversation about the man condemned to death who is then reprieved. Here again, the effect of this account disarms the hostility of the Epanchin sisters toward the prince, whom they initially look on with suspicion, as a kind of interloper. Third, there is the prince's advice to Adelaida Epanchina, who is seeking a subject for a picture, to paint the face of a condemned man awaiting execution.

The prince then describes all the feelings of the condemned man awaiting execution. All these episodes evoke some aspects of Dostoevsky's own mock execution.

An important thematic motif is expressed at the end of the story about the man who is condemned to death by a firing squad and then reprieved. During the period of waiting, before he knows that he will live, he feels that if life were to be granted to him, he would not waste a moment of it. In other words, he would live as if every moment were to be his last. But Prince Myshkin then admits that the person, about whom he was telling the story, did not live up to this resolution. Alexandra Epanchina counters with: "Well . . . so it seems it's impossible really to live 'counting each moment.'" Prince Myshkin replies: "So it seemed to me also . . . and yet somehow I can't believe it," stressing the conflict between reason and moral ideal. Myshkin is here clearly talking about himself and defining what he feels to be his own mission. Even if the person in Myshkin's story did not live up to this dream, there is no doubt that Myshkin himself wants to do so. The prince—who has just emerged from a state of epileptic unconsciousness that can be felt almost as a reprieve from death—on reentering the world wants to live in the eschatological tension that was (and is) the soul of the primitive Christian ethic, its totally selfless *agape* that takes no account of time.

In part one, in general, the relation of Myshkin to the other characters is clear. Each of them is acting in terms of some egoistic drive—whether vanity, greed, ambition, sensual desire. The appearance of Myshkin, like the appearance of Christ in the world, has the effect, momentarily, of bringing them to a moral awareness of their selfishness and stirring in them a sense of a higher moral, or unselfish, order. In each case he ignites in them some spark of a better or, at least, less entirely self-centered self.

Of course, he has the most effect on Nastasya Filipovna, who is suffering from the deepest wounds and is consumed by self-hatred and self-loathing because of her degradation. This has been brought on against her own will because she was seduced by Totsky almost as a child. She is eaten up with contempt and hatred for those who have ruined her life and are now trying to buy and sell her like a piece of chattel.

The key to her character is given in the description of her picture and what Myshkin says about it (part 1, chapter 3): "It's a proud face, arrogant, but I wonder if she is kind-hearted." Nastasya's fierce pride makes it impossible for her to forgive those who have ruined her life. Worst of all, she cannot forgive herself, even though she is a victim, and there is something masochistic and suicidal in her behavior. Nastasya came to St. Petersburg to confront Totsky and his scheme to marry her off to Ganya Ivolgin while himself marrying one of the Epanchin sisters. Pure at heart but furious at Totsky and eager to avenge her outward dishonor, she ends up destroying the prince, whom she likes and who, in some respects, is the embodiment of her own dream. When at her soiree, she asks the prince to decide whether or not she should marry Ganya Ivolgin, the prince offers her his hand and fortune. But Nastasya publicly turns him down. She cannot tolerate the idea of taking advantage of Prince Myshkin and his innocence. Unable to break the grip of what Dostoevsky calls the egoism of suffering, this subtle and complex form of egoism causes her a great deal of suffering and will ultimately destroy her.[17] But it often bears a positive value for Dostoevsky

17. "Egoism of suffering" is an expression Dostoevsky used in the novel he wrote just after returning from Siberia, *The Insulted and Injured*: "She enjoyed her own pain by the egoism of suffering, if I may so express it. This aggravation of suffering and this rebelling in it I could understand; it is the enjoyment of man, of the insulted and the injured, oppressed by destiny, and smarting under the sense of injustice."

when it leads the character, as in Raskolnikov, to a moral reevaluation and change, or as in *Notes from Underground*, when it is the only way of preserving a sense of moral responsibility. But Nastasya's suffering, however, does not lead to any sort of moral self-purification. Her egoism of suffering does not have that effect; it is a means of taking revenge, not of inner transformation (part 1, chapter 16). The reference to hara-kiri at the end of part one serves as yet another example of the insulted party taking revenge on oneself.

It is not clear, at the end of part one, just how lasting and powerful will be the impact of Prince Myshkin on the others. There seems to be a foreshadowing, in the story of Marie, that he may be able to bring peace to the tormented souls in Petersburg as he had done in the Swiss village. Since Dostoevsky was so uncertain about the progress of the novel, he may well have initially considered this a possibility. But it can also be seen, taking place among children, as already setting up a contrast to what takes place later on. The "two loves" motif of the story already suggests the conflict between Christian love (Nastasya) and earthly love (Aglaia) in which Myshkin will be caught. It is a very subtle touch to have the children think that these two kinds of love are the same.

Reading Dostoevsky's letters and notebooks (after he sent the publisher part one of *The Idiot*), makes it quite clear that he was continually grappling with and worrying about the problem of what was to come next. And so these middle sections have a lot of isolated scenes, some of which are marvelous, such as the party scene at the end of part one, chapter 16, when Nastasya throws money into the fire. Characters like General Ivolgin, the wonderful mythomaniac, would be hard to find an equal elsewhere except perhaps in Shakespeare's Falstaff. The story of General Ivolgin and Napoleon during the occupation of Moscow by

Napoleon (part 4, chapter 6) is a satirical takeoff that shows how brilliantly amusing Dostoevsky can be. But such scenes do not seem to have much inner connection with each other. However, they possess three narrative strands that alternate with each other.

One strand is the Myshkin-Nastasya-Rogozhin intrigue, which seemed to be the main line of action but which also vanishes for long periods. A second strand is the Aglaia-Myshkin relationship, with Radomsky as the romantic competitor. A third strand comprises all the scenes involving the Young Nihilists, Ippolit, the comic capers of Lebedyev, a kind of parody of the main religious themes, also to be found in medieval drama and Shakespeare, and the wonderful tall stories of General Ivolgin.

Part two begins with a curious intermezzo of five chapters, in which Prince Myshkin (as well as others, like Rogozhin and Lebedyev) is seen in a new light. The prince, in this interim of six months, is supposed to have undergone an important evolution, and there is now an extremely important shift in the way the prince is presented. In part one his epilepsy was treated as an incidental fact of his life, not linked with his character in a substantive way. It forms the background that helps to motivate his innocence, but it does not play a significant role.

It is when the prince emerges from his epilepsy that he awakens to the ecstatic apprehension of life. Indeed, his apprehension of death has become the source of his love of life, and the attempt to live each moment as an eternity seems to have nothing specific to do with his epilepsy. But in part two we see that his hopes of transforming those with whom he comes into contact (Nastasya and Rogozhin) are presented as a consequence of his experience of the epileptic aura and also as a sublime illusion. It is when he is undergoing the effects of this aura that he thinks: "Compassion is the chief and maybe the only law of human existence" (part 2, chapter 5).

The importance of this shift is that it now shows the prince's highest values to be irreconcilably in opposition with the conditions of normal earthly life. For now, his highest values are shown to be rooted in, and traced to, his experience "of peacefulness and of ecstatic devotional merging with the highest synthesis of life" that he feels in the epileptic aura.[18] But he also knows that "stupefaction, spiritual darkness, idiocy stood before him as a glaring consequence of these 'higher moments.'" These higher moments thus have no place in the world and can only lead to disaster. This shift in motivation may explain the Gothic tonality of these chapters, unlike anything before, and also the strange conversation about faith with Rogozhin. Nothing earlier had indicated that the prince was a character to be troubled by such questions.

This exchange between Prince Myshkin and Rogozhin, provoked by Holbein's painting *The Dead Christ in the Tomb*, culminates in four anecdotes. Taken together, their point of view seems to be that the human (but most strongly exhibited by the Russian) need for faith and for the moral values that faith sustains transcends both the plane of rational reflection and that of empirical evidence. Religious faith is independent of morality on the social level. The murderer utters a prayer before he kills. What is important is not that the religious gesture doesn't stop the crime but that the criminal continues to make it all the same. This means that the criminal has not become totally unrepentant, that for him the crime does not fundamentally undermine the higher moral order.

18. Ibid.

FIGURE 5. Hans Holbein the Younger, *The Dead Christ*, 1521. Tempera on panel. Kunstmuseum, Basel, Switzerland/Bridgeman Images.

"The essence of religious feeling," Prince Myshkin says to Rogozhin, "is not suitable for reasoning, crimes or misdemeanors, or any kind of atheism" (part 2, chapter 4). Dostoevsky is here separating faith from social morality. In his book *Fear and Trembling*, the Danish religious philosopher Søren Kierkegaard analyzes God's commandment to Abraham to sacrifice his son Isaac—a commandment that Abraham obeys until an animal is sacrificed instead—and called a situation of this sort—the command of God to commit a crime—the teleological suspension of the ethical.[19] The two situations evoked are not the same, but they resemble each other in illustrating the irrationality of religious faith, which in both cases is affirmed and split off from any social morality justified by reason. Applying this notion to Prince Myshkin himself, the reader observes that Myshkin's practical failure ought not to weaken the values of Christian love and religious faith that he embodies.

The action of these chapters, which serves as a kind of coda to the main intrigue of part one, exemplifies the altered role of the prince. He tries to intervene in the drama of Rogozhin and Nastasya and to save the crazed beauty from destroying herself. But even though Rogozhin knows that the prince's love is compassionate, not carnal, the prince's power over Nastasya interferes with Rogozhin's desperate and hopeless need to possess her in spirit as well as in body. And this sequence ends with the attempted murder, foiled by Prince Myshkin's first epileptic fit since leaving the hospital in Switzerland.

The middle section of the book is filled with a plethora of incidents that are only loosely (if at all) connected with the main plot lines of the novel. But it's not too hard to see the thematic significance of the characters as they reflect one or another as-

19. Nastasya Filipovna's surname, Barashkova, translates as "of a lamb."

pect of the prince himself, thereby creating the notion of quasi doubles in this larger framework. Lebedyev is a comic analogue of the prince, who parodies both his compassion and his irrational faith. He prays every night for Madame du Barry in sympathy because of her suffering before being guillotined during the French Revolution, and his funny, but also gruesome, story of the repentant cannibal in the Middle Ages makes the same point as the prince's anecdote about faith. Lebedev does so in a hilarious parody of legal rhetoric to prove that faith, which in this case inspires moral conscience, finally makes the cannibal confess (part 3, chapter 4).

The episode involving the Young Nihilists is another illustration of the same point. They appear to be attacking morality, but at the same time, they insist that the prince behave like "a man of conscience and honor" (part 4, chapter 1). They believe in egoistic self-interest but assume that their own motives are pure and untainted. They believe instinctively (or subconsciously) in the moral values they appear to have discarded and lambaste the prince for not living up to them.

Out of the group of Young Nihilists, Ippolit emerges as a much more important figure who is not comic at all, or if so, only in terms of a modern black comedy (for example, Samuel Beckett) than of anything comparable in nineteenth-century literature. Ippolit is very important as the first of Dostoevsky's metaphysical rebels, who revolt not against the moral norms of society (as does Raskolnikov) but against the injustices of the human condition itself. A suggestion that originated in Makar Devushkin's despairing words at the end of *Poor Folk* becomes here a full-fledged theme. And Ippolit revolts against a world in which evil exists, not as a result of any sort of social arrangement that can be remedied, but because of the sickness and death that has condemned him in particular to an early grave. In this respect he is an opposing "double" of the prince because the two share Myshkin's ecstatic sense of the immeasurable value of life. But for this very reason, Ippolit is all the more embittered that God has doomed him to be deprived of that life so young.

The function of Ippolit in the novel is both to challenge Prince Myshkin's ultimate Christian values and to bring out their necessity by contrast. His "necessary explanation" (part 3, chapter 5) (which is unnecessary, of course) contains all the main features of Prince Myshkin's beliefs; but these are combined with an opposite human attitude. Ippolit doesn't dismiss the notion of God, as a confirmed atheist would; instead, he attacks God because of the world he has created. Unable to conquer his doubts, he believes in the miracle of the Resurrection. This is brought out by his reaction to the same Holbein painting that had earlier led the prince to reaffirm his faith to Rogozhin. But for Ippolit the painting represents the definitive triumph of a dead and soulless nature over Christ and over any belief in a life after death.

Even though Ippolit is a precursor of Ivan Karamazov, he is quite clearly a much simpler figure. Ippolit's revolt springs from his own suffering; it is not the result of being converted to any abstract theory. Also, the egoism he displays is a naïve and touching, not embittered, kind. Nor is Ippolit's revolt linked with any views that could have a harmful social effect (despite his affiliation with the Young Nihilists). Ivan Karamazov's revolt against God, on the other hand, leads him to dissolve all moral-social norms.

Dostoevsky's attitude toward Ippolit is quite complex, a mixture of deep pity and sad admonition. Myshkin tells Radomsky that nobody has a right to criticize Ippolit and one should ask for his forgiveness because he is condemned to death before his time. But he, Ippolit, too must conquer his own egoism (an "egoism of suffering" similar to Nastasya's) and forgive others. In one of the most poignant moments of the book (part 4, chapter 5), the prince tells him: "Pass by and forgive us our happiness." The scenes with Ippolit, in the complexity of their tonality, are among the most original that Dostoevsky ever wrote.

If there is any major plotline in the book after part one, it is the prince's romance with Aglaia Epanchina. It is this romance, finally, that brings on the catastrophe. Aglaia is a normal, high-spirited young woman, who is attracted by the moral beauty of the prince's beliefs and behavior. But she can't help viewing them (in the only terms she is familiar with) through her aristocratic background and assimilation of European cultural ideals. She, however, confuses the Russian kenotic Christ with the conquering crusaders of the Catholic West, and she sees Prince Myshkin as a warrior and a hero who combines spiritual faith and temporal power. Very few commentators have noticed the incongruity of the "poor knight" image with what Myshkin actually is. But Dostoevsky brings it out in several ways, climaxing in Myshkin's tirade against Catholicism exactly at the point where he is going to be introduced as Aglaia's fiancé. And the way in which Dostoevsky marries off Aglaia in the epilogue seems to strengthen this incongruity.[20]

The last part of the book is given over to the conflict between Aglaia and Nastasya over the prince and his helplessness in the face of their conflicting demands. This is the point at which the "two loves" motif comes to a climax, and in which Prince Myshkin is simply trapped between the two. Each woman has a differing but equally powerful claim on his devotion, and it is impossible for him to give up either his compassion for Nastasya or his

---

20. She marries a Catholic, allegedly a member of the Polish nobility, who is in reality penniless, and who ends up taking all of Aglaia's money.

passion for Aglaia. In ordinary terms, the prince just goes to pieces, but Dostoevsky here is dramatizing the profoundest level of his whole conception of the prince as the embodiment of his own religious problematic.

Dostoevsky was, of course, perfectly well aware of how the prince would be regarded from an ordinary point of view, and he tries to take this into account in several ways. One is by allowing Radomsky to comment on the prince's strange behavior. The other is through his narrative technique. The narrator of the book abandons Prince Myshkin by saying that he finds him incomprehensible, and he ends up reporting only on the rumors about the prince that were circulating. The prince has, in other words, passed beyond the ordinary sphere of social comprehension implied by a conventional narrative. It is useful to refer again to Kierkegaard: Abraham, too, in *Fear and Trembling*, is thought to be mad when he goes out to obey the commandment of God, which no one else has heard. Lebedyev wants to commit Myshkin to an asylum and brings a doctor. We are reminded that when St. Paul spoke to the Greeks, they were also supposed to have considered his teachings a scandal because they were so irrational.

The book ends with the famous death scene, whose effect, Dostoevsky said, he could guarantee. The prince returns to the darkness of epilepsy, consoling Rogozhin, the murderer, whose crime was partly caused by Myshkin's epileptic illusion, and whose life seemingly led to nothing but catastrophe. Nonetheless, the book ends on a note indicating that, at least with some people, Myshkin's moral inspiration continues to have an effect.

The Idiot was not a great success when it was published, though it gradually attracted a growing number of readers. Dostoevsky himself complained that it was written under conditions that made it impossible for him to polish and develop his ideas properly. His two important succeeding novels after this, *A Raw Youth* and *The Devils*, did not deal with the same issues, but the second of these is among his best works. It is only with *The Brothers Karamazov* that he returned to the same theme on a much larger scope; it is the greatest novel he ever wrote, and he tried to give his religious theme a more positive resolution than he did in *The Idiot* through the figure of Father Zossima. But, of course, it was impossible for him to accomplish this completely because it was impossible to portray the theme of immortality within the confines of the realistic novel.

CHAPTER 7

The Brothers Karamazov

~

Lecture 1

Dostoevsky wrote two major novels during the 1870s. One was *A Raw Youth*, sometimes also called *The Adolescent*, which was published in the leading populist journal of the period. This fact is important for interpreting the book as a work of art as well as for its interest in relation to Dostoevsky's shift of feelings in relation to the young radicals.

A Raw Youth is written as a picaresque novel and is the autobiography of a young man just growing up. Like a picaresque hero, he is the illegitimate son of a nobleman and a serf woman; he uses his father's name but grows up on the edge of society as a social outcast. This leads him to invent all sorts of plans to gain revenge on those who insult him, and he even becomes involved with a revolutionary group. But the most important aspect of the book is the boy's relation to his father, Versilov, who is a more humane and moderate example of the Stavrogin-type. By this I mean the Russian-European type who represents Dostoevsky's rage at the effects of Western culture on the Russian upper class.

Versilov does all sorts of senseless things *à la* Stavrogin—or seemingly so, since the senselessness is a result of the moral disorientation caused by the loss of religious faith. But, in line with the shift in the climate of ideas toward what might be called an atheistic religiosity, what we now see in Versilov is a longing for faith. Instead of the defiance, the challenge to a supreme arbiter of mankind who lays down the rules of good and evil—what we find in Versilov is a nostalgia for what has been lost—and a desire for its return. But Versilov himself in the novel is not able to accomplish this return to faith, even though he does not end in suicide like Stavrogin. Instead, Versilov makes a partial return but not completely and lives with his mistress, his former serf and household maid, as a semi-invalid. But the symbolism of his union with the people is obvious.

The main character is the raw youth, of course, and it is his relation with his father that is the core of the book. So we see here Dostoevsky already beginning to write a novel about a Russian family—and a relationship between fathers and sons. But this is no longer treated in the ideological terms of the relations between the generations of the 1840s and the 1860s as in *The Devils.* Now the focus is not so much on the ideology as such but on the problem of the moral values that the fathers of the older generation were handing on to their children. Dostoevsky began to feel that the real problem for Russians was the breaking up of the family, the existence of what he called "accidental families," and therefore the lack of any related tradition of moral values that would help the children with some stability and security as they are starting out in life. This will, of course, be shown more starkly in the *The Brothers Karamazov.*

In *A Raw Youth,* the character of the son actually has two fathers. One is Versilov, the Russian European, and the other is an old Russian peasant, Makar Ivanovich Dolgoruky, who is a religious pilgrim. He is not the biological father of the youth but his spiritual father—as Father Zossima will be to Alyosha Karamazov. It is Makar Ivanovich who imparts to the son the religious and moral-social values of the Russian people, and it is these values that help the son, Arkady, to overcome the various temptations by which he is beset. Here once again the symbolism of the structure of the action is perfectly obvious. The values that the son needs to enable him to confront the trials and temptations of life—which in this case have a strong sexual component—can only come from his assimilation of the people's truths and not from the Western-European culture of his biological father, Versilov. This was a message that would have had a considerable appeal to Dostoevsky's young populist readers, who did not think that the Western conception of the ideal society of the future should be taken as a guide by Russians. And while they would not have accepted Makar Ivanovich as an image or icon of the values of Russian peasant life (he was too religious for them), Dostoevsky very cleverly used such a character to appeal to their own idealization of the Russian peasantry.

A Raw Youth is not among Dostoevsky's greatest novels, though attempts have been made in recent years to reevaluate it more positively. I tend to agree with those who think it inferior as a whole, though it was, after all, written by Dostoevsky at the height of his power and does contain marvelous pages. But I think that the place of publication led Dostoevsky to hold himself back, as it were, and not to allow his imagination to work at its usual stretch. What is wrong with the book, it seems, is that it is full of melodramatic incidents and rather hackneyed plot elements that are not raised in Dostoevsky's usual fashion by the philosophical and moral-religious elements of the conception. The level of the action remains on the social and psychological plane, except in one or two instances, and is not lifted up to a higher region of artistic-ideological expression. The reason for this was that Dostoevsky did not wish to antagonize the editors of the *Notes of the Fatherland*, whose readership was the liberal-minded intelligentsia, by too obviously introducing a religious theme, and so he held himself in check. He was not really able to write freely, and this accounts for the relative failure of the book.

Dostoevsky later spoke of *A Raw Youth* as a kind of first sketch or draft of *The Brothers Karamazov*; he said that he was glad he had not undertaken to give his theme of accidental families and fathers and children its full expression at that time. We can now see why he made this remark. Meanwhile, after *A Raw Youth*, he took several years off from writing novels and devoted himself to his *Diary of a Writer*. But this was not really as much of a diversion from his artistic path as might appear at first sight. For Dostoevsky all this time was thinking of his theme of fathers and children, of the confusion and chaos in Russian life caused by the lack of any firm moral values handed on from fathers to their families, and he was gathering material for his next creation. In one of his letters, this is exactly how he spoke about his *Diary of a Writer*—he called it an "artistic laboratory" for his next work, and many of the elements he used in the novel can be linked with articles he wrote in the *Diary*.

It would take too long to go through them all, but we can find material in the *Diary* related to the theme of children in the novel; to Ivan Karamazov's rebellion against God; to the Legend of the Grand Inquisitor and the view of Catholicism given there; to some of the details about cruelty to children given in Ivan's speeches, which were taken from court cases that Dostoevsky wrote about; and the court scenes of the novel itself, where the defense attorney is modeled on an actual famous defense attorney about whom Dostoevsky writes in the *Diary*. Many of these motifs can be found in Dostoevsky's earlier work, but the *Diary* gave him the opportunity to refine and polish them in relation to actual material taken from Russian life of the period.

All this finally culminated in the composition of *The Brothers Karamazov*, which is Dostoevsky's greatest work and one of the summits of the novel as a form. If *A Raw Youth* was uneven and uncertain, then with *The Brothers Karamazov* Dostoevsky came into his own and succeeded in giving expression to his great theme: the conflict between reason and Christian faith. Dostoevsky had never before succeeded in giving this theme so majestic and powerful a form, and his book takes its place among the greatest creations of the Western literary tradition. One thinks of Dante's *Divine Comedy*, Milton's *Paradise Lost*, Shakespeare's *King Lear*, Goethe's *Faust*—these are the comparisons that spring to mind for *The Brothers Karamazov*.

The characters in *The Brothers Karamazov* have a monumental quality that is worth dwelling on for a moment because the beginning of the novel is not really so very different from Dostoevsky's earlier ones. He keeps the usual emphasis on action seized at some high point of crisis—there is the usual emphasis on scene rather than on description or lengthy character analysis—and his characters are projected through long monologues as people who reveal themselves and are highly aware of their own natures. But in addition to all this, Dostoevsky now presents his characters in terms of a much larger symbolic background than earlier. They are not only social ideological types of the Russian intelligentsia or of Russian society, but now they are also seen as representative of age-old historical forces and conflicts.

Ivan Karamazov can be seen as a more developed type of the same kind of character as Ippolit in *The Idiot*. He is no longer in revolt against God because of his own suffering but because of the existence of a world in which the unexpiated suffering of little children exists. This already broadens Ivan's dimension as a character. But in addition, his own ideas and values are now expressed in terms of legends and miracle plays of the Middle Ages, the eschatological myth of the returning Christ, the *auto-da-fé* of the Spanish Inquisition, and the New Testament story of Christ's temptation by Satan.

Dmitry is surrounded by the atmosphere of Schiller's Hellenism and the struggle of the Olympian gods with the dark and bestial forces that had ruled mankind before their coming. Father Zossima is the direct inheritor of the crucial heritage of one of the most cherished traditions of the Eastern Church. Alyosha is placed in this same religious context, and his crisis of doubt recalls that of *King Lear* and *Hamlet* since it calls the entire order of nature into question. And it is resolved by a cosmic intention of the secret beginning linking the earth and the starry heavens. Even Old Karamazov is extended in this way, being called a Roman of the period of decadence and also being linked by his anecdotes with the eighteenth century of Voltaire and Catherine the Great. It is this extension of symbolic range that gives *The Brothers Karamazov* the monumental quality we find in it and inevitably reveals the kind of comparisons we have mentioned.

Now, the theme of the book, as we already mentioned, is the conflict between reason and faith—but in the terms that this conflict had taken on for Dostoevsky in the 1870s. The populist ideology no longer claimed Christian values, but it claimed the Christian faith. So the conflict between reason and faith, as Dostoevsky saw it, was now posed much more sharply and clearly in Russian culture than had been the case in the past. Dostoevsky's earlier novels, in a certain sense, had defended Christian values themselves, and the question of faith itself had remained in the background. But now it comes forward as a dominating theme of *The Brothers Karamazov*. This conflict between reason and faith is dramatized with incomparable force and sublimity in books 5 and 6 of part two of the novel. The famous idea—the logical center of the book—includes the Legend of the Grand Inquisitor, a story within the narrative that

Ivan tells Alyosha. These chapters usher in Ivan's revolt against a Christian God, the indictment of Christ himself in the legend for having imposed a burden on mankind too heavy to bear; and then, in reply, Father Zossima preaching of the necessity for a faith in God and a love for one's fellow man in transcending the bounds of human reason.

Dostoevsky once said that, in reality, the whole novel was a reply to the Legend of the Grand Inquisitor.[1] And I think this furnishes the reader with a very valuable clue to the interpretation of the work, for it provides us with a sense of the interconnection that he felt between the various parts and interweaving plotlines. This connection is based on the analogy between the human situation expressed in Ivan's poem and the conflicts of all the important characters. What we see in the legend is an expression of Ivan's "Euclidian understanding," his contempt for the spiritual limitations of the mass of mankind. He cannot understand a surrender to the Christian hope justified by nothing except the radiant image of the God-man, Christ, and he believes that humanity will surrender its freedom for the promise of earthly bread.

The remainder of the book is an answer to the legend because, in one way or another, all of the characters are required to make a similar leap of faith in someone or something beyond themselves. They are all called on to transcend the bounds of their own egoism in some act of self-surrender. This theme is expressed by Ivan in religious and theological terms. With the other characters it is expressed in terms of their own dominating drives and impulses, their own personal form of egoism. It is in this

1. For additional information and analysis, see Joseph Frank's *Dostoevsky: The Mantle of the Prophet, 1871–1881* (Princeton, NJ: Princeton University Press, 2002), 571.

context—differing according to each character but all inter-woven together in the novel—that each is called on to accom-plish an act of moral self-transcendence. Such an act is irrational in the sense that it conflicts with immediate self-interest in some way. Reason and egoism are identical, and therefore the surrender of self-interest in one form or another goes against rea-son, as it was defined by the Russian radicals of Dostoevsky's lifetime, and involved a leap of faith similar to the one de-manded by Ivan's legend on the religious plane.

I think that such a pattern can be found in most of the the-matic plotlines of the book and even in the organization of its most obvious structural features. Take, for example, the central plot on its most literal level. This concerns a trial for murder. Dmitry is not guilty of the murder of his father, but on the basis of all legal reasoning, an overwhelming case has been compiled against him. All the circumstantial evidence points in his direc-tion. But the fact is that he is innocent. And only those who go against all the appearances of reason—only those who are will-ing to take his word on faith, only those who follow the intuition of their heart about him, not the so-called facts—only they know the truth. Dmitry is thus convicted falsely. All the appara-tus of legal rationality isn't enough to know the real truth, which comes through the heart and feelings. This is how the main theme appears in its most obvious form.

The opening section of the book introduces all four of the cen-tral characters and gives us our first glimpse of them. Old Karamazov is a familiar Dostoevskian type: the vengeful buffoon who began life by being humiliated but then turns into a tyrant and bully himself the moment he gets power. In this case he also exhibits an uncontrollable sensuality that is something new for this type. He is a father of this accidental family, whose members have received no values of any kind from him and have each gone off in their own way.

At the same time, Dostoevsky indicates that even in the depths to which Old Karamazov had sunk, he is not merely a monster of the flesh. When his first wife dies, he shouts with joy and also weeps. And years later he suddenly gives a thousand rubles to the monastery to pay for requiems for her soul. But he drinks furiously and insults the monks nonetheless. So even he, too, is caught in some sort of struggle between a lower and higher principle in his being, which is revealed in various ways—most notably, in his emotional dependence on Alyosha.

Dmitry and Ivan are characterized more briefly than Old Karamazov or Alyosha in this opening section, but each represents one aspect of their father. Dmitry has inherited his sensuality, while Ivan resembles him in the sharpness of his intellect. Ivan also has the typical traits of the Dostoevsky dreamer figure, the morose young intellectual brooding over the world's problems. But a deeper glimpse is given into Ivan by the mention of his article about the ecclesiastical courts. Ivan's position was so ambiguous that both sides believed he was advocating their point of view. And this of course exhibits both his attraction to the Church and its values, as well as his resistance against it.

Alyosha is the brother who receives the most attention here, for several reasons. He was, in the first place, to be the hero of the series of novels about the family that Dostoevsky planned to write. Also, Dostoevsky was at great pains to make the reader feel that Alyosha was not a fantastic or eccentric character like Prince Myshkin. Dostoevsky wanted to present a positive figure who was normal and perfectly healthy, not an invalid or epileptic, and yet who was totally committed, heart and soul, to the Christian faith. Alyosha, we see, is also called "an early lover of humanity"

and "a youth of our last epoch" (book 1, chapter 4), who was passionately seeking truth and justice. And he adds that if Alyosha
had stopped believing in God and immortality, then he would
immediately have become an atheist and socialist. The same
qualities that led Alyosha to Zossima could have led him to revolution if he had lost his faith. This conception of Alyosha has
becomes possible because of the new populist acceptance of
Christian moral values in the faith that we see exhibited by the
Russian peasant women in book one. And such a scene, in its
verisimilitude—for scenes of this kind certainly took place in famous monasteries—was meant for populist eyes, to show them
the true force of the Russian people and their commitment to
the religion of their forefathers.

It is also in relation to Alyosha that the main theme of the
novel begins to appear. For the narrator mentions Alyosha's faith
in miracles, though he is also called "more of a realist than anyone" (book 1, chapter 5). But we see here that such realism is
carefully separated from faith or belief. The difference between
the two is that true faith is not dependent on anything external,
material, visible, tangible, empirical. Faith colors and determines
our apprehension of the empirical world, and not the other way
around. This passage anticipates Alyosha's spiritual crisis over the
decay of Father Zossima's body, which is just one of the ways in
which Dostoevsky projects his major theme. This may be defined, in one of its aspects, as the total opposition of true faith
to anything external to itself, any search for confirmation, justification, or external support for what should be a pure act of
inner affirmation.

This theme of the necessity for a faith that needs no support
from the empirical and tangible is then illustrated, in a back-
handed way, in the conversation of Alyosha and his father. Old
Karamazov tries to conquer his fear of hell by trying to imagine

it is a physical place full of machinery of punishment. Not being able to do so, he pretends it doesn't exist. But this only strains the limits of his Euclidian understanding. And in general, we can say that faith is something that will always surpass such Euclidian understanding, which excludes all experience that transcends the natural. The same kind of understanding appears, in different ways, in Old Karamazov, Madame Khokhlakova, Smerdyakov, Father Ferapont (he is a special problem), and, finally, in the Devil who appears to Ivan.

The action of the book begins in book two, where we learn that the enmity between Dmitry and his father is not only over money but also over Grushenka. Various aspects of advanced rational views are presented in the liberal Miusov and in Madame Khokhlakova. Her conversation with Father Zossima again picks up the theme of faith. How is one to prove immortality? And Zossima answers that no proof is possible. Only active love can bring faith, and in this way we see the connection of the book's two main themes. What I called earlier the transcendence of the self and egoism is the only way that faith can be obtained if it is lacking.

The character of Ivan is also developed further in the discussion involving his article about church and state. The reader can see that Ivan argues on behalf of the church absorbing the state within itself, which would mean that the law of love would rule every area of secular and social life. There would be no law in the strict sense, no external forceful constraint, but the free action of Christian conscience operating as a moral force. This would truly be the establishment of the kingdom of God on earth. Ivan's advocacy of this goal indicates how strongly he responds to the appeal of the Christian ideal in its loftiest form.

At the same time, though, he also argues that all this depends on a belief in God and immortality. Without such a belief, the law of nature becomes the direct opposite of the religious law, and only egoism becomes lawful. Only Christian faith supports the law of love in the world. The fact that Ivan argues both these positions shows the extent of his inner conflict and of course foreshadows the Legend of the Grand Inquisitor. And Father Zossima, listening to him, sees the anguish of Ivan's spiritual condition. Zossima tells Ivan that he is playing with the martyrdom of his own indecision and despair. And Ivan is so moved by what Zossima says about his (Ivan's) "exalted heart able to suffer through this ordeal" that he reverently kisses the priest's hand and asks for his blessing.

Dmitry is also developed further in book two, and we begin to see here that he is more than just a rowdy brawler. He has a longing for "seemliness" and he is, unlike Ivan, genuinely religious. He is also capable of remorse, as we see in his repentance over the way he has behaved toward Captain Snegiryov. But Dmitry also has an uncontrollable temper. And it is after witnessing Dmitry in one of his rages that Father Zossima bows down at his feet.

This book is rounded off by the depiction of Alyosha's relation with Lise Khokhlakova. This may be a preparation for the succeeding novels that Dostoevsky did not live to write. Lise may be compared to Ippolit in *The Idiot* as a character. Her own illness makes her perverse and hateful, but she is also pathetic because of her youth and innocence. Her relation with Alyosha parallels that of Ivan with Katerina and Dmitry with Grushenka. Her character is certainly also meant as a reflection on the kind of life and education she has been given by her frivolous mother.

This section is then rounded off by the contrast between Alyosha and Rakitin. He is also a novice in the monastery but has been converted to atheism, science, and positivism. He believes that humanity will find in itself the power to live for virtue even without believing in immortality—and hence without God or Christ. But Rakitin himself always acts from the most selfish motives, and he represents the possibility that Ivan invoked when he said that without God and immortality, the law of nature (egoism) would prevail in the world.

The next two books, three and four, show Alyosha making a round of visits, through which we get to know a number of characters more fully. Here, too, we also get the history of Smerdyakov, who is probably the illegitimate son of Old Karamazov. We also learn about the old man's living arrangements—important for the unraveling of the main plot action—and of Old Karamazov's relation with the servant Grigory. This is important because we see here how even someone as cynical and debased as Old Karamazov cannot really exist without appealing himself emotionally to the law of love that he desires. For he relies on Grigory's faith and devotion—that is, he trusts him implicitly, appealing to Grigory's loyalty, a loyalty that is rooted in the servant's Christian faith, even though he abhors the behavior of his master. So we see how even Old Karamazov takes an irrational leap of faith in the devotion of Grigory and relies on this, not only practically but as a kind of consolation "in moments of drunkenness, when he was overcome by superstitious terror and a moral convulsion which almost, so to speak, physically shook his soul."

The next important sequence includes the scenes between Alyosha and Dmitry. Here we have another example of the sudden growth of a character in scope and dimension. For in Dmitry's "Confession of a Passionate Heart," we begin to see him in a new light. From the rowdy young officer and resentful brawler he becomes a figure whose every word vibrates with turbulent and impassioned poetry. We have earlier seen Dmitry as a character whose dissolute life has not yet destroyed his moral sense. And now Dostoevsky elevates both these sides of his personality to a kind of mythical stature. He quotes poetry, which raises the disgust at his own degradation into a struggle of mankind to sublimate and purify its animal lusts and instincts. Dmitry is incapable of curbing and suppressing these instincts, but he longs for some change within nature that will enable him to attain self-respect. And this is exactly how he will achieve it—on the level of passion, of a passion for Grushenka that turns lust into genuine love. But for the moment he is still bewildered, and as he says, "I don't know whether I am going to shame or to light and joy." For man harbors both the ideal of the Madonna and the ideal of Sodom in his soul. This, of course, is a statement of Dmitry's problem, which is that of the struggle against sensuality and the flesh. The ideal of the Madonna is not that of the flesh suppressed or denied, but ennobled and transfigured by genuine love.

It is against this background that the story of Dmitry's relationship with Katerina unfolds. He had set out to seduce her solely out of wounded vanity, not out of physical passion, and their relationship thus turns into a contest for domination. Katerina's only response is to treat Dmitry in such a way as to drive home to him his moral inferiority, and this she does by her magnanimity. Life had become intolerable to him under the burden of her "gratitude." And so when he meets the sensuous and tantalizing Grushenka, he is completely swept away.

The next four chapters focus attention on Smerdyakov, whose character inspires pity and repulsion at the same time. He is, of course, a kind of double of Ivan and anticipates the appearance of the Devil in Ivan's hallucination further on in the book. He is depicted as a character completely devoid of any natural feelings of gratitude or obligation. And he is also one of the "rationalists" who people the book. All these "rationalists," of course, are in one way or another caricatures of Ivan's tortured moral nihilism. Smerdyakov is also a social type that Dostoevsky felt was on the rise in Russia and was cannon fodder for revolution. The uprooting of the peasants from their old culture, and their exposure to the new ideas of rationalism, would have an explosive effect on Russian life.

Book three also contains scenes involving Katerina and Grushenka, and these are continued in book four, where Ivan breaks with Katerina Ivanovna as decisively as Dmitry had done earlier. What Ivan says about Katerina—that she is incapable of any but lacerated love—also applies to himself. Katerina is in some sense a double of Ivan, and I think that her function, besides her role in the plot, is to allow Dostoevsky to bring out Ivan's characteristics in more human terms. We see him largely transposed in terms of ideological argument and poetic symbol. But the resemblance between the characters of Katerina and Ivan gives us some of the traits of his personality more directly. Ivan's intellectual arrogance and pride prevent him from surrendering to the mystery of faith, and Katerina's inability to love anyone except herself is rooted in these same human qualities.

Book four also contains the portrait of Father Ferapont, who is the opposite of Zossima in the monastery. His function, I think, is to set off the relative enlightenment of Zossima, whom Dostoevsky did not want to be confused with the harsher traditions of Russian monasticism. But on a deeper thematic level, Ferapont is also part of the attack on rationalism made in the book. Even though he is a priest and believes in the supernatural, he is yet a rationalist because of the literalism of his faith in the supernatural. He imagines it materializing in all its specificity, not as a spiritual but a literal reality, and in this way he resembles Old Karamazov. His religion is confirmed by material proofs, and is thus not faith in the true sense—which must be pure of any admixture of confirmation by fact. Faith must be sustained only by itself.

The dialogical center of the novel, as Dostoevsky rightly said himself, is contained in books five and six. To this should also be added book seven, which contains the account of Alyosha's spiritual crisis and its resolution. The opposing pro and contra of the debate between Ivan and Zossima is framed by the Alyosha theme, which serves as a resolution of their opposition.

The three chapters in which Ivan expresses his rebellion against God's world are similar to those that we saw in the case of Dmitry. Here again we get that sudden vertical expansion of a character through which he suddenly seems to grow in scale, though the change is not as startling in the case of Ivan as with Dmitry. But we don't have time to dwell too much on this change. Let's focus on the legend itself, which contains the ideological core of the book. Whole volumes have been written about it, and we can hardly begin to scratch the surface here.

Lecture 2

In this lecture I have the impossible job of saying something intelligent about Dostoevsky's last great novel in the space of a couple of hours. *The Brothers Karamazov* is a colossal work that ranks among the very greatest creations of literature, and we think, when speaking of it, of the most towering moments of the whole history of Western art: the *Oresteia*, Dante, Michelangelo, *King Lear*, Beethoven's Ninth. Dostoevsky's work seems to take its place with such creations rather than with an ordinary novel, good though it may be. Even its great rival, Tolstoy's *War and Peace*, does not have the force and the impact of *The Brothers Karamazov*—at least in my opinion. As a result, it seems almost a sin to try and say anything about it in such a short space of time. But what I want to do is to give the readers some general ideas about it, which may help them in their own study.

Thus an approach to the book starts in the analysis that I gave in the previous lecture on the changed cultural situation. Put in the simplest terms, one can say that Dostoevsky was no longer arguing with the radicals on behalf of Christian ethical values. He was now arguing on behalf of the Christian faith itself. The radicals themselves had come around to accepting the usual values of Dostoevsky and Christianity and were idealizing the peasant and his life—which were rooted in a simple and naïve belief in God and Christ. Here was the point at which Dostoevsky now felt that he could possibly appeal to the radical intelligentsia on their own terms and show them the shortcomings of their point of view. For how could one accept the Christian values of peasant life without their basis in God? This is where Dostoevsky starts from, though he raises the issue to a point that rivals the most sublime expressions of the paradoxes of the Christian faith, and of faith in general: the existence of evil in a world created by an all-powerful deity who is worshipped as the source of goodness.

If we look at the novel as a whole, huge though it is, can we find a central point of view that might enable us to get its main theme in proper focus? I think there is, and it is tied up with the problem I already stated. For we must always keep in mind that, in this book, Dostoevsky is trying to show that humankind is constantly drawn to confront and acknowledge the ultimate mystery and irrationality of human life and of the human personality. Any attempt to stay within the bounds of reason and

common sense, so as to evade and deny this mystery or irrationality, leads to irreconcilable inner conflict and ultimately to
human self-destruction. And once the point is reached at which
a person does confront this ultimate mystery and irrationality,
the only adequate response one can make to it is that of faith in
God and Christ. But it must be faith in the same sense: that is,
a faith willing to accept itself as irrational and paradoxical. It
must not search for support in anything material and tangible.
Christ is rational in the broad sense, and faith must, in effect, rely
only on itself and the strength of its own conviction.

This is, I believe, the basic idea of the book; and if one approaches the book in this way, one will see how it is carried out
in most (if not all) of the major incidents described in the book.
For example, if we go back to the major plotline of the book, in
the simplest sense, it concerns a trial for murder. As we said before, Dmitry is not guilty of the murder of his father, and it is
only on the basis of legal reasoning, on the basis of all the evidence, that the overwhelming case against him points to his guilt.
But the fact is that he is innocent. And only those who go against
all the appearances of reason, only those who are willing to take
his word on faith, those who follow the intuitions of their heart—
not the so-called facts that the legal process produces and
would have us believe—they alone know the truth. Thus Dmitry is convicted falsely. And all the apparatus of legal rationality
isn't enough to arrive at the truth.

So we might reply to this that it is, after all, a jury of peasants
who convict Dmitry. How does this fit with the theme that the
peasants are the repositories of that irrational faith in whose
name Dostoevsky is supposedly writing? The answers can be
given here. One is that the peasants are confused by the alien
forms of Western legal rationality (as a result of the Judicial
Reform of 1864) in terms of which the trials are conducted.

Dostoevsky wrote in an article in the early 1870s that this Western legal rationality often led to miscarriages of justice in the new courts. However, a deeper and more subtle reason emerges if we examine the argument of the defending attorney. For there we see that the peasants actually are defending the same thematic points as those who believe that Dmitry is innocent. The attorney argues that Dmitry's father, Old Karamazov, was not really a father because of his cruelty and neglect of his children; from any rational point of view of justice, his murder would have been entirely excusable. This denies the irrational bond of unconditional love between father and son that constitutes the basis of the family— one that is rooted in Christian faith. This is the value that the peasants are defending, and in convicting Dmitry wrongly they confirm the thematic heart of the novel.

Another example of this general pattern can be seen in the situation involving Alyosha and the decomposition of the body of Father Zossima. At first sight, this may seem difficult to integrate with my general theme. After all, what Alyosha was waiting for was a miracle—that Father Zossima's body, because he was saintly, would not decay as rapidly as that of an ordinary mortal. Such a tradition was deeply rooted in the Orthodox Church and goes even farther back to the earliest periods of Christianity. And what is a miracle if not a manifestation of the irrational that confirms and justifies religious faith? But this latter point is precisely the issue.

Alyosha's expectation of a manifest miracle, an infringement of the order of nature, is really a temptation of the Devil. It is one of the temptations that Christ resists in the Legend of the Grand Inquisitor. This need to see a material miracle, a miracle, as it were, that would satisfy any reasonable man about Zossima's sanctity is precisely Alyosha's temptation. It is the way that rationality is translated into his theological terms. For faith, in

Dostoevsky's terms, needs (or should need) nothing beside itself. Its purity is enhanced by the fact that it is assumed freely and quite independent of all proofs and rewards. In this sense, Dostoevsky's religious ideal is quite close to Kierkegaard's, which also stresses that faith is a transcendence of all the criteria of rationality—in other words, a commitment to the absurd—though, of course, Dostoevsky would not have used such terminology.

These two examples illustrate the central pattern of the book, and it is one that is repeated on many different levels. Let's look at the members of the Karamazov family, for example. In each of them we can see some aspect of the ultimate irrationality of human personality, which illustrates the need for and the power of a faith that transcends reason.

Old Karamazov lives almost completely on the level of his lusts and appetites and is capable of the most shameless behavior. On the level of conscious convictions, he is a convinced eighteenth-century materialist who turns such ideas into an excuse for his own villainies. And yet we see that the thought of hell bothers him a little bit, though he tries to reason it away with sophistries about the material impossibility of such a place as hell, where the hooks can be located, and so on (book 1, chapter 4). This is the equivalent of Alyosha's desire for a material miracle and also the semisatirical portrait of Father Ferapont. He is a kind of saintly equivalent at one extreme of Old Karamazov on the other.

The point is, though, that Old Karamazov knows that hell is not a physical place but a state of being, and in spite of himself, he is inwardly terrified by the possibility of the supernatural. This is why he needs Alyosha, who is the only person in the world who doesn't condemn him. Alyosha's attitude is the secular and temporal equivalent of the relation with the supernatural that Old

Karamazov longs for and fears will not be forthcoming. This doesn't stop him from behaving as he does, but it indicates that even so gross a materialist still has a spiritual and moral dimension. He secretly longs for what he denies and violates at the same time, and thus he demonstrates the irrational case of freedom in the human personality that is irreducible to any rational set of categories.

We find the same point illustrated in another way in the character of Dmitry. Dmitry has inherited all the sensuality of his father but with a much higher degree of moral self-awareness to counterbalance it. While it is impossible to tear Old Karamazov away from his lusts, Dmitry oscillates, as he says himself, between the ideal of the Madonna and that of Sodom. Dmitry is not an atheist or materialist, but he is, all the same, plunged in the materialism of his sensuality and his passions. His rationalizing, as we may call it, is not intellectual but exists on the level of the passions, in the sense that he does not believe it possible for him to escape from the grip of his vices. Given his nature, temperament, and past life, there is no reason to expect he can ever change. But in the course of events, his relationship with Grushenka moves from the purely sensual to genuine love, tenderness and devotion, or from the material to the spiritual. In this way, we can say that we see the irrational—which in Dostoevsky is always identical with the spiritual—triumphing over the material, which in Dostoevsky again is always identified with the rational. Whether or not we accept such equations, they did exist for Dostoevsky and help us to grasp some of the relations of analogy that exist in *The Brothers Karamazov*.

Ivan is not a passionate heart like Dmitry; rather, he inherits the cold and sarcastic intellect of his father. His conflict is thus expressed in ideological terms. We first hear about him in relation to his theory of the relation of church and state. Now we know that in Dostoevsky's thought the state is the principle of the material rather than the spiritual, founded on power and force rather than on love. The Church, on the other hand—at least ideally—is based on the brotherhood of man in Christ, and on mutual love (the triangle thus excludes Roman Catholicism, which grasped after temporal power). The state, moreover, incarnates the principle of reason since it dispenses justice (and justice is rational) according to merit and punishes according to blame. The Church is the spiritual and the irrational because its punishment is inward and moral (if it punishes at all) and would only consist in outlawing the criminal from the community of love. For the state to be absorbed in the Church would mean the triumph of the spiritual and of love over might and power.

Ivan speaks in favor of the Church absorbing the state even though he does not believe in God. This illustrates the split in his personality that eventually leads to his breakdown. He appreciates all the importance of the moral, the spiritual, and the irrational, and feels the need for it emotionally himself, but is unable to embrace it fully because of the overweening rationality of his intellect.

There is, of course, a fourth son, Smerdyakov, who must also be taken into account. He plays a double role in the book. In the first place, he is Dostoevsky's image of what might happen when the kind of rationalism represented by Ivan comes into contact with the mentality of the peasant (Smerdyakov) and is reduced, as it were, to its lowest common denominator. Smerdyakov, from his earliest childhood, had shown an incapacity to be moved by the imaginary and the spiritual, and he always adopts a strictly practical and utilitarian point of view. He resembles Old Karamazov and Father Ferapont in this respect, and he parodies their interaction in another key. But of course, he's also a parody of Ivan, and he plays somewhat the same role in relation to him as Svidrigailov does to Raskolnikov in *Crime and Punishment*. Smerdyakov carries to its logical conclusions the practical consequences of Ivan's ideas that Ivan chooses not to face himself. Since Ivan is a self-conscious humanitarian whose heart is torn by human suffering and who knows no Superman theory to overcome his scruples, it would have been impossible to allow him to commit the murder himself.[2]

Another quasi double for Ivan is Katerina Ivanovna. She represents not so much Ivan's ideas as his character deprived of the inner conflict that betrays his awareness of the limitation of his own ideas and values. Katerina possesses all of Ivan's intellectual pride and egoism, and her so-called charity toward others is really, like his, just another manifestation of his egoism. Just as her female vanity makes it impossible for her to surrender to Ivan, whom she really loves, so his intellectual vanity makes it impossible for him to surrender to Christ, whom he really loves. We shall come back to this point in a moment. But just let me point out in passing other uses of this quasi-double technique. The relation of Madame Khokhlakova to Father Zossima is a kind of parody of that of Alyosha to Zossima. And the relationship of Lise and Alyosha parallels that of Katerina and Ivan.

But now let's turn to the section of the book that Dostoevsky himself said contained its essence—that is, books five and six. This portion contains the Legend of the Grand Inquisitor and Zossima's reminiscences and thoughts. The ideological core of

2. *Übermensch*/Superman/Overman, a term coined by Friedrich Nietzsche in *Thus Spoke Zarathustra* (1883–1885) to describe someone willing to break any societal law for the betterment of humanity.

the book is concentrated here, and whole volumes have been written particularly about the legend. We won't go into its genesis, which is very important and can be easily discovered through a number of articles in *The Diary of a Writer*.[3] But the assimilation that Dostoevsky makes in the legend between socialism and Roman Catholicism has caused a lot of confusion. Why, if his main enemy was the socialist radicals, did he incarnate the principle of tyranny and despotism in the Grand Inquisitor of Roman Catholicism? One answer often given relates to the influence of Schiller's *Don Carlos*.[4] This response is probably true, but superficial. Another, a little deeper, is that the Slavophils and Dostoevsky saw both Roman Catholicism and socialism as part of the same ideology of temporal power. Socialism, a French creation (see Fourier), was merely the atheistic version of the Catholic ideal that Prince Myshkin had attacked in *The Idiot* as having betrayed Christ. On a deeper level, perhaps, while the legend is only Ivan's creation, it is he who speaks for the radicals and who sees their ideal embodied in the great representative

3. From a book review Joseph Frank wrote for *Inflamed, A Writer's Diary*, vol. 1, 1873–1876, by Fyodor Dostoevsky, trans. and ann. Kenneth Lantz (Evanston, IL: Northwestern University Press, 1993): "*Diary of a Writer*, the least known of all [Dostoevsky's] books, contains some of his most moving autobiographical pages, and records his contacts with, and reactions to, other Russian writers such as Nekrasov, Leskov, Belinsky and Tolstoy, and it helps illuminate an entire stretch of Russian cultural history." *London Review of Books* 15, no. 23 (December 2, 1993): 18–19.

4. In Friedrich Schiller's dramatic poem *Don Carlos* (1783–1787), the title character is the son of the Spanish king, Philip II. He is in love with Elisabeth, the eldest daughter of the French king, Henry II. For political reasons, Elisabeth is forced to marry Don Carlos's father. Unable to be with Elisabeth, Don Carlos decides to leave Spain. When he visits Elisabeth to say goodbye, King Philip II has him arrested and turns him over to the Inquisition.

of tyranny over the soul of humanity. The prophetic power of Dostoevsky here is really staggering when one thinks of the later history of the Russian radicals and the Revolution of 1917, which continued the tradition to which Ivan (if only partially) adhered.

In any case, a reader needs to keep in mind this point: it is Ivan, and not Dostoevsky or another character, who wrote the legend. And he does so in a special frame of mind: he has just broken with Katerina, and at last he feels free; he tells Alyosha that he has a primitive, instinctual, and irrational love of life. This is the reflection in Ivan of the elemental vitality of the Karamazovs. But he has also lost faith in life itself, all taste for life, and is living, as it were, out of the instinct of his youth rather than out of real joy in life. The problem for Ivan is to find a reason for continuing to live beyond the period when his instinct will carry him along.

Now the reason for his disillusionment with life is precisely the irrational suffering of humanity. But it is very important to notice the point of view from which Ivan describes this suffering. It is the point of view of someone who is moved by the suffering but who loathes humanity at the same time. For the suffering he describes is caused by people's evil propensities that are part of human nature. Thus Ivan is himself detached from humanity and feels superior to it, like the Grand Inquisitor, but he also pities it for its suffering. And he insists that this dichotomy makes sense to his Euclidian understanding, that is, an understanding that attempts to measure the mystery of evil and suffering in terms of reason. So long as one stays on this level, Ivan's arguments are logically irrefutable. And it is part of Dostoevsky's genius as a writer that he did not hesitate to give Ivan's position the strongest possible presentation. He was perfectly right to say, as he did in his *Diary*, that nowhere in European literature could one find so powerful an expression of atheism as in the chapter "Ivan's Rebellion."[5]

But then this is followed by the legend, which is one of the most beautifully subtle creations in all of literature. The aim of the legend is to undermine the rational arguments of Ivan by showing that they are really based on his contempt for mankind, as was mentioned earlier. It is contempt mixed with love, but contempt all the same. Since Ivan is the author of the poem, it reflects all the conflict of his personality. On the one hand, we have the radiant figure of the returning Christ, which reveals all of Ivan's genuine longing for the spiritual and the transcendent, for the community of love and faith in Christ. This is an expression of the same impulse in Ivan that leads him to defend the thesis of the Church absorbing the state. But then we see the arrival of the Inquisitor, who arrests Christ and explains in his monologue that there is no room for him any longer.

The reason is that the Church has established a rule over man's spirit based on the external forces of miracle, mystery, and authority—that is, an earthly bread, a material reward, an external manifestation of power. All this is done for man's happiness, and it works—thus satisfying the demands of his reason. But Christ, as we see, had rejected this kind of power when it had been offered him by Satan. Christ did not want to base his authority over man on material proofs of his power of one sort or another but solely on the free gift of man's love based on faith—not on anything material and hence rational.

So we see how this view of Christ fits in with the general pattern of interpretation I have tried to use for the book. All the

---

5. *Diary of a Writer* in F. M. Dostoevskii, *Polnoe sobranie sochinenii v tridtsati tomakh*, ed. V. G. Bazanov et al. (Leningrad: Nauka, 1980), 27.

major plotlines dramatize, in some analogical fashion, the same conflict between the material, the sensual, and faith, love, trust. And so we see how the Grand Inquisitor scorns Christ for rejecting these temptations on the ground that man is too weak to bear the burden of this moral freedom. For this requires man to choose to follow Christ in total freedom and solely out of love. So we see that though the Grand Inquisitor loves mankind in his own way (not like Ivan), he also feels contempt for it. Or, at least, he wishes to deny mankind moral autonomy, which is the basis of human personality for Dostoevsky.

Now, we can see a little more clearly in what respect this legend undermines Ivan's logically irrefutable argument rejecting God because of the suffering of little children. This argument comes from Ivan's Euclidian understanding, that is, his desire to have the goodness of God make sense in some rational fashion. But the universe does not make sense in this way precisely because God wanted man to choose Christ in perfect freedom and entirely independently. God did not want a choice to be made because man knew in advance that God was all powerful and all good. God's love for man is displayed by the fact that he believes, unlike Ivan and the Inquisitor, in man's capacity to choose Christ freely. In other words, God endowed man with moral autonomy and freedom of will because he believed in man's capacity to accept God against all appearance and against all rationality. Here again we are very close to Kierkegaard's views.

This is one way, in which, as it were, the legend answers Ivan's arguments. God's love of man is displayed precisely by endowing him with the capacity for evil—that is, free will. The Grand Inquisitor, on the other hand, has assumed the Christian mantle while denying people the very essence of Christian faith, as Dostoevsky saw it. This is an implicit admission that mankind will only accept salvation from Christ and will never surrender the realm of the spirit and moral autonomy, even though it may be deceived by the Church. The false Christ must speak in the name of the true one if he wishes to obtain a hearing. And this is meant to apply to the Russian radicals of Dostoevsky's time, who rejected the supernatural Christ but accepted the moral values of his teaching. The final kiss that Christ gives the Inquisitor, and that Alyosha gives Ivan, is the kiss of forgiveness and of all forgiving love. For both the Inquisitor and Ivan do love and pity suffering mankind in their own way—just not enough to trust it with freedom. This kiss, in my view, represents Dostoevsky's own attitude to the new radicals, whom he was prepared to forgive but not to accept—and whose lack of true faith could turn them into terrible tyrants.

Selected Adaptations for Film and TV of the Novels Covered in the Lectures

Novel Title	Movie Title, Director, Country, Year
Poor Folk	*My Neighbor Martika*, Marc Windon, France, 2016 *Bednye lyudi*, Bahodyr Adylov and Dzhahangir Kasymov, Uzbekistan, 1992 *Oameni Sarmani*, Ion Barna, Romania, 1969 *Les pauvres gens*, Antoine Mourre, France, 1938
The Double	*The Double*, Richard Ayoade, UK, 2014 *Enemy*, Denis Villeneuve, Canada, Spain, 2014 *Partner*, Bernardo Bertolucci, Italy, 1968 *Neprijatelj*, Zivojin Pavlovic, Serbia, 1965
The House of the Dead	*Z mrtvého domu*, Stéphane Metge, France, Japan, 2008 *From the House of the Dead*, Brian Large, Austria, 1992 *Myortvy dom*, Vasilii Fyodorov, USSR, 1932
Notes from Underground	*Notes from Underground*, Beau Han Bridge, Canada, 2019 *Johnny Walker*, Kris De Meester, Anton Scholten, Belgium, USA, Netherlands, 2015 *Inside*, Zeki Demirkubuz, Turkey, 2012 *Feljegyzesek az egerlyukbol*, József Sipos, Hungary, 2011 *J'irai cracher sur vos tongs*, Michel Toesca, France, 2005 *Notes from Underground*, Gary Walkow, USA, 1995 *Jour et nuit*, Jean-Bernard Menoud, France, 1986 *Aikalainen*, Timo Linnasalo, Finland, 1984 *El Hombre del Subsuelo*, Nicolás Sarquís, Argentina, 1981

Continued on next page

Novel Title	Movie Title, Director, Country, Year
	Bobo la tête, Gilles Katz, France, 1980
Crime and Punishment	*Crime and Punishment*, Vladimir Sokolsky, Matthew Hroch, Canada, 2019
	Bridge of Sleep, Oktane Brahmani, Oktay Baraheni, Iran, 2018
	Crime and Punishment, Andrew O'Keefe, Australia, 2015
	Student, Darezhan Omirbaev, Kazakhstan, 2012
	Norte: Hangganan ng Kasaysayan, Lav Diaz, Philippines, 2013
	Nina, Heitor Dhalia, Brazil, 2004
	Crime and Punishment, Menahem Golan, USA, Russia, Poland 2002
	Crime and Punishment, Julian Jarrold, UK, 2002
	Crime and Punishment, Piotr Dumala, Poland, 2002
	Crime and Punishment, Joseph Sargent, USA,1998
	Sin Compasión, Francisco J. Lombardi, Peru, Mexico, France, 1994
	Schuld und Sühne, Andrzej Wajda, Germany, 1992
	Rikos ja Rangaistus, Aki Kaurismäki, Finland, 1983
	Crime and Punishment, Michael Darlow, UK, 1979
	Jurm Aur Sazaa, Nisar Ahmad Ansari, India, 1974
	Neramu Siksha, K. Vishwanath, India, 1973
	Zlocin i kazna, Sava Mrmak, Yugoslavia, 1972
	Crime et châtiment, Stellio Lorenzi, France,1971
	Crime and Punishment, Lev Kulidzhanov, USSR, 1970
	Rikos ja rangaistus, Mauno Hyvönen, Finland, 1967
	Delitto e castigo, Anton Giulio Majano, Italy, 1963
	Raskolnikoff, Franz Peter Wirth, West Germany, 1959
	Pickpocket, Robert Bresson, France, 1959
	Crime and Punishment, Denis Sanders, USA, 1959
	El Gharima waal ikab, Ibrahim Emara, Egypt, 1957
	Crime et châtiment, Georges Lampin, France,1956
	Raskolnikow, Curt Goetz-Pflug, Frank Lothar, West Germany, 1953
	Crimen y castigo, Fernando de Fuentes, Mexico, 1951
	Brott och straff, Hampe Faustman, Sweden, 1945
	Crime and Punishment, Josef von Sternberg, USA, 1935
	Crime et châtiment, Pierre Chenal, France, 1935
	Paper Parinam, India, 1924
	Raskolnikow, Robert Wiene, Germany, 1923
	Prestuplenie i nakazanie, Ivan Vronsky, Russia, 1913
	Prestuplenie i nakazanie, Vasily Goncharov, Russia, 1909

Novel Title	Movie Title, Director, Country, Year
The Idiot	*Idioot*, Rainer Sarnet, Estonia, 2011
	Idiot, Vladimir Bortko, Russia, 2003
	Down House, Roman Kachanov, Russia, 2001
	Navrat Idiota, Sasa Gedeon, Czech Republic, 1999
	Nastasja, Andrzej Wajda, Japan and Poland,1994
	The Idiot, Mani Kaul, India, 1992
	L'amour braque, Andrzei Zulawski, France,1985
	Der Idiot, Rolf von Sydow, West Germany, 1968
	L'idiot, Andre Barsacq, France, 1968
	Au hazard Balthazar, Robert Bresson, France, 1966
	L'idiota, Giacomo Vaccari, Italy, 1959
	Idiot, Ivan Pyryev, USSR,1959
	Hakuchi, Akira Kurosawa, Japan,1951
	L'idiot, Georges Lampin, France, 1946
	Irrende Seelen, Carl Froelich, Denmark, 1921
	Il principe idiota, Eugenio Perego, Italy, 1920
	L'idiota, Salvatore Aversano, Italy, 1919
	Idiot, Pyotr Chardynin, Russia, 1910
The Brothers Karamazov	*Brothers Karamazov*, Jun'ichi Tsuzuki, Japan, 2013
	Son of Man, Janek Ambros, USA, 2011
	Bratya Karamazovy, Vladimir Bortko, Russia, 2009
	Bratya Karamazovy, Yury Moroz, Russia, 2009
	The Karamazov Brothers, Petr Zelenka, Czech Republic, 2008
	Inquisition, Betsan Morris Evans, UK, 2002
	Mal'chiki, Yuriy Grigoryev, USSR, 1990
	Le grand inquisiteur, Raoul Sangla, France, 1979
	Bratya Karamazovy, Kirill Lavrov, USSR, 1969
	I fratelli Karamazov, Sandro Bolchi, Italy, 1969
	Les frères Karamazov, Marcel Bluwal, France, 1969
	Gebroeders Karamazow, Anton Peters, Belgium, 1968
	Brothers Karamazov, Richard Brooks, USA, 1958
	I fratelli Karamazoff, Giacomo Gentilomo, Italy, 1947
	Der Mörder Dimitri Karamasoff, Erich Engels, Fyodor Ozep, Germany, 1931
	Die Brüder Karamasoff, Carl Froelich, Dimitri Buchowetzki, Germany, 1921
	Brothers Karamazov, Lawrence B. McGill, USA, 1917
	Bratya Karamazovy, Viktor Tourjansky, Russia, 1915.

APPENDIX II

Joseph Frank's Dostoevsky

~

Have a prolegomenous look at two quotations. The first is from Edward Dahlberg, a Dostoevsky-grade curmudgeon if ever in English there was one:

> The citizen secures himself against genius by icon worship. By the touch of Circe's wand, the divine troublemakers are translated into porcine embroidery.[1]

The second is from Turgenev's *Fathers and Sons*:

> "At the present time, negation is the most useful of all—and we deny—"

> "Everything?"

> "Everything!"

> "What, not only art and poetry . . . but even . . . horrible to say . . ."

> "Everything," repeated Bazarov, with indescribable composure.

As the backstory goes, in 1957 one Joseph Frank, then thirty-eight, a Comparative Lit professor at Princeton, is preparing a

---

1. From "Can These Bones Live?" in *The Edward Dahlberg Reader*, New Directions, 1957.

lecture on existentialism, and he starts working his way through Fyodor Mikhailovich Dostoevsky's *Notes from Underground*. As anyone who's read it can confirm, *Notes* (1864) is a powerful but extremely weird little novel, and both these qualities have to do with the fact that the book is at once universal and particular. Its protagonist's self-diagnosed "disease"—a blend of grandiosity and self-contempt, of rage and cowardice, of ideological fervor and a self-conscious inability to act on his convictions: his whole paradoxical and self-negating character—makes him a universal figure in whom we can all see parts of ourselves, the same kind of ageless literary archetype as Ajax or Hamlet. But at the same time, *Notes from Underground* and its Underground Man are impossible really to understand without some knowledge of the intellectual climate of Russia in the 1860s, particularly the frisson of utopian socialism and aesthetic utilitarianism then in vogue among the radical intelligentsia, an ideology that Dostoevsky loathed with the sort of passion that only Dostoevsky could loathe with.

Anyway, Professor Frank, as he's wading through some of this particular-context background so that he can give his students a comprehensive reading of *Notes*, begins to get interested in using Dostoevsky's fiction as a kind of bridge between two distinct ways of interpreting literature, a purely formal aesthetic approach vs. a social-dash-ideological criticism that cares only about thematics and the philosophical assumptions behind them.[2] That interest, plus forty years of scholarly labor, has

---

2. Of course, contemporary literary theory is all about showing that there's no real distinction between these two ways to read—or rather it's about showing that aesthetics can pretty much always be reduced to ideology. For me, one reason Frank's overall project is so worthwhile is that it shows a whole different way to marry formal and ideological readings, an approach that isn't nearly as abstruse and (sometimes) reductive and (all too often) joy-killing as literary theory.

yielded the first four volumes of a projected five-book study of Dostoevsky's life and times and writing. All the volumes are published by Princeton U. Press. All four are titled *Dostoevsky* and then have subtitles: *The Seeds of Revolt, 1821–1849* (1976); *The Years of Ordeal, 1850–1859* (1984); *The Stir of Liberation, 1860–1865* (1986); and this year, in incredibly expensive hardcover, *The Miraculous Years, 1865–1871*. Professor Frank must now be about seventy-five, and judging by his photo on *The Miraculous Years*'s back jacket he's not exactly hale,[3] and probably all serious scholars of Dostoevsky are waiting bated to see whether Frank can hang on long enough to bring his encyclopedic study all the way up to the early 1880s, when Dostoevsky finished the fourth of his Great Novels,[4] gave his famous Pushkin Speech, and died. Even if the fifth volume of *Dostoevsky* doesn't get written, though, the appearance now of the fourth ensures Frank's status as the definitive literary biographer of one of the best fiction writers ever.

** Am I a good person? Deep down, do I even really want to be a good person, or do I only want to *seem* like a good person so that people (including myself) will approve of me? Is there a difference? How do I ever actually know whether I'm bullshitting myself, morally speaking? **

In a way, Frank's books aren't really literary biographies at all, at least not in the way that Ellmann's book on Joyce and Bate's on

---

3. The amount of library time he must have put in would take the stuffing out of anybody, I'd imagine.

4. Among the striking parallels with Shakespeare is the fact that FMD had four works of his "mature period" that are considered total masterpieces—*Crime and Punishment, The Idiot, Demons* (a.k.a. *The Demons*, a.k.a. *The Devils*, a.k.a. *The Possessed*), and *The Brothers Karamazov*—all four of which involve murders and are (arguably) tragedies.

Keats are. For one thing, Frank is as much a cultural historian as he is a biographer—his aim is to create an accurate and exhaustive context for FMD's works, to place the author's life and writing within a coherent account of nineteenth-century Russia's intellectual life. Ellmann's *James Joyce,* pretty much the standard by which most literary bios are measured, doesn't go into anything like Frank's detail on ideology or politics or social theory. What Frank is about is showing that a comprehensive reading of Dostoevsky's fiction is impossible without a detailed understanding of the cultural circumstances in which the books were conceived and to which they were meant to contribute. This, Frank argues, is because Dostoevsky's mature works are fundamentally ideological and cannot truly be appreciated unless one understands the polemical agendas that inform them. In other words, the admixture of universal and particular that characterizes *Notes from Underground*[5] really marks all the best work of FMD, a writer whose "evident desire," Frank says, is "to dramatize his moral-spiritual themes against the background of Russian history."

Another nonstandard feature of Frank's bio is the amount of critical attention he devotes to the actual books Dostoevsky wrote. "It is the production of such masterpieces that makes

5. Volume III, *The Stir of Liberation,* includes a very fine explicative reading of *Notes,* tracing the book's genesis as a reply to the "rational egoism" made fashionable by N. G. Chernyshevsky's *What Is to Be Done?* and identifying the Underground Man as basically a parodic caricature. Frank's explanation for the widespread misreading of *Notes* (a lot of people don't read the book as a *conte philosophique,* and they assume that Dostoevsky designed the Underground Man as a serious Hamlet-grade archetype) also helps explain why FMD's more famous novels are often read and admired without any real appreciation of their ideological premises: "The parodistic function of [the Underground Man's] character has always been obscured by the immense vitality of his artistic embodiment." That is, in some ways Dostoevsky was too good for his own good.

Dostoevsky's life worth recounting at all," his preface to *The Mi-raculous Years* goes, "and my purpose, as in the previous volumes, is to keep them constantly in the foreground rather than treating them as accessory to the life per se." At least a third of this latest volume is given over to close readings of the stuff Dostoevsky produced in this amazing half decade—*Crime and Punishment, The Gambler, The Idiot, The Eternal Husband,* and *Demons.*[6] These readings aim to be explicative rather than argumentative or theory-driven; their aim is to show as clearly as possible what Dostoevsky himself wanted the books to mean. Even though this approach assumes that there's no such thing as the Intentional Fallacy,[7] it still seems prima facie justified

---

6. This last one Frank refers to as *The Devils.* One sign of the formidable problems in translating literary Russian is the fact that lots of FMD's books have alternative English titles—the first version of *Notes from Underground* I ever read called itself *Memoirs from a Dark Cellar.*

7. Never once in four volumes does Professor Frank mention the Intentional Fallacy [7(a)] or try to head off the objection that his biography commits it all over the place. In a way this silence is understandable, since the tone Frank maintains through all of his readings is one of maximum restraint and objectivity: he's not about imposing any particular theory or method of decoding Dostoevsky, and he steers clear of fighting with critics who've chosen to apply their various axes' edges to FMD's work. When Frank does want to question or criticize a certain reading (as in occasional attacks on Bakhtin's *Problems of Dostoevsky's Poetics,* or in a really brilliant response to Freud's "Dostoevsky and Parricide" in the appendix to Volume I), he always does so simply by pointing out that the historical record and/or Dostoevsky's own notes and letters contradict certain assumptions the critic has made. His argument is never that somebody else is wrong, just that they don't have all the facts.

What's also interesting here is that Joseph Frank came of age as a scholar at just the time when the New Criticism was becoming entrenched in the US academy, and the good old Intentional Fallacy is pretty much a cornerstone of New Criticism; and so, in Frank's not merely rejecting or arguing against the IF but proceeding as if it didn't even *exist,* it's tempting to imagine all kinds of marvelous patricidal currents swirling around his project—Frank giving an enormous silent raspberry to his old teachers. But if we remember that New Criticism's removal of the author from the

by Frank's overall project, which is always to trace and explain the novels' genesis out of Dostoevsky's own ideological engagement with Russian history and culture.[8]

** What exactly does "faith" mean? As in "religious faith," "faith in God," etc. Isn't it basically crazy to believe in something that there's no proof of? Is there really any difference between what we call faith and some primitive tribe's sacrificing virgins to volcanoes because they believe it'll produce good weather? How can somebody have faith before he's presented with sufficient reason to have faith? Or is somehow *needing* to have faith a sufficient reason for having faith? But then what kind of need are we talking about? **

---

interpretive equation did as much as anything to clear the way for poststructural literary theory (as in e.g. Deconstruction, Lacanian psychoanalysis, Marxist/Feminist Cultural Studies, Foucaultian/Greenblattian New Historicism, & c.), and that literary theory tends to do to the text itself what New Criticism had done to the author of the text, then it starts to look as if Joseph Frank is taking a sharp early turn away from theory[7(b)] and trying to compose a system of reading and interpretation so utterly different that it (i.e., Frank's approach) seems a more telling assault on lit theory's premises than any frontal attack could be.

[7(a)] In case it's been a long time since freshman lit, the Intentional Fallacy = "The judging of the meaning or success of a work of art by the author's expressed or ostensible intention in producing it." The IF and the Affective Fallacy (= "The judging of a work of art in terms of its results, especially its emotional effect") are the big two prohibitions of objective-type textual criticism, especially the New Criticism.

[7(b)] (Said theory being our own age's big radical-intellectual fad, rather as nihilism and rational egoism were for FMD's Russia.)

8. It seems only fair to warn you, though, that Frank's readings of the novels are extremely close and detailed, at times almost microscopically so, and that this can make for slow going. And also that Frank's explications seem to require that his reader have Dostoevsky's novels fresh in mind—you end up getting immeasurably more out of his discussions if you go back and actually reread whatever novel he's talking about. It's not clear that this is a defect, though, since part of the appeal of a literary bio is that it serves as a motive/occasion for just such rereading.

To really appreciate Professor Frank's achievement—and not just the achievement of having absorbed and decocted the millions of extant pages of Dostoevsky drafts and notes and letters and journals and bios by contemporaries and critical studies in a hundred different languages—it is important to understand how many different approaches to biography and criticism he's trying to marry. Standard literary biographies spotlight an author and his personal life (especially the seamy or neurotic stuff) and pretty much ignore the specific historical context in which he wrote. Other studies—especially those with a theoretical agenda—focus almost exclusively on context, treating the author and his books as simple functions of the prejudices, power dynamics, and metaphysical delusions of his era. Some biographies proceed as if their subjects' own works have all been figured out, and so they spend all their time tracing out a personal life's relation to literary meanings that the biographer assumes are already fixed and inarguable. On the other hand, many of our era's "critical studies" treat an author's books hermetically, ignoring facts about that author's circumstances and beliefs that can help explain not only what his work is about but why it has the particular individual magic of a particular individual writer's personality, style, voice, vision, etc.[9]

** Is the real point of my life simply to undergo as little pain and as much pleasure as possible? My behavior sure seems to

---

9. That distinctive singular stamp of himself is one of the main reasons readers come to love an author. The way you can just tell, often within a couple paragraphs, that something is by Dickens, or Chekhov, or Woolf, or Salinger, or Coetzee, or Ozick. The quality's almost impossible to describe or account for straight out—it mostly presents as a vibe, a kind of perfume of sensibility—and critics' attempts to reduce it to questions of "style" are almost universally lame.

indicate that this is what I believe, at least a lot of the time. But isn't this kind of a selfish way to live? Forget selfish—isn't it awful lonely? **

So, biographically speaking, what Frank's trying to do is ambitious and worthwhile. At the same time, his four volumes constitute a very detailed and demanding work on a very complex and difficult author, a fiction writer whose time and culture are alien to us. It seems hard to expect much credibility in recommending Frank's study here unless I can give some sort of argument for why Dostoevsky's novels ought to be important to us as readers in 1996 America. This I can do only crudely, because I'm not a literary critic or a Dostoevsky expert. I am, though, a living American who both tries to write fiction and likes to read it, and thanks to Joseph Frank I've spent pretty much the whole last two months immersed in Dostoevskynalia.

Dostoevsky is a literary titan, and in some ways this can be the kiss of death, because it becomes easy to regard him as yet another sepia-tinted Canonical Author, belovedly dead. His works, and the tall hill of criticism they've inspired, are all required acquisitions for college libraries . . . and there the books usually sit, yellowly, smelling the way really old library books smell, waiting for somebody to have to do a term paper. Dahlberg is mostly right, I think. To make someone an icon is to make him an abstraction, and abstractions are incapable of vital communication with living people.[10]

---

10. One has only to spend a term trying to teach college literature to realize that the quickest way to kill an author's vitality for potential readers is to present that author ahead of time as "great" or "classic." Because then the author becomes for the students like medicine or vegetables, something the authorities have declared "good for them" that they "ought to like," at which point the students' nictitating membranes come down, and everyone just goes through the requisite motions of criti-

** But if I decide to decide there's a different, less selfish, less lonely point to my life, won't the reason for this decision be my desire to be less lonely, meaning to suffer less overall pain? Can the decision to be less selfish ever be anything other than a selfish decision? **

And it's true that there are features of Dostoevsky's books that are alien and off-putting. Russian is notoriously hard to translate into English, and when you add to this difficulty the archaisms of nineteenth-century literary language, Dostoevsky's prose/dialogue can often come off mannered and pleonastic and silly.[11]

---

cism and paper-writing without feeling one real or relevant thing. It's like removing all oxygen from the room before trying to start a fire.

11. . . . especially in the Victorianish translations of Ms. Constance Garnett, who in the 1930s and '40s cornered the Dostoevsky & Tolstoy–translation market, and whose 1935 rendering of *The Idiot* has stuff like (scanning almost at random):

"Nastasya Filippovna!" General Epanchin articulated reproachfully.

. . . "I am very glad I've met you here, Kolya," said Myshkin to him. "Can't you help me? I must be at Nastasya Filippovna's. I asked Ardelion Alexandrovitch to take me there, but you see he is asleep. Will you take me there, for I don't know the streets, nor the way?"

The phrase flattered and touched and greatly pleased General Ivolgin: he suddenly melted, instantly changed his tone, and went off into a long, enthusiastic explanation.

And even in the acclaimed new Knopf translations by Richard Pevear and Larissa Volokhonsky, the prose (in, e.g., *Crime and Punishment*) is still often odd and starchy:

"Enough!" he said resolutely and solemnly. "Away with mirages, away with false fears, away with spectres! . . . There is life! Was I not alive just now? My life hasn't died with the old crone! May the Lord remember her in His kingdom and—enough, my dear, it's time to go! Now is the kingdom of reason and light and . . . and will and strength . . . and now we shall see! Now we shall cross swords!" he added presumptuously, as if addressing some dark force and challenging it.

Umm, why not just "as if challenging some dark force"? Can you challenge a dark force without addressing it? Or is there in the original Russian something that keeps the above phrase from being redundant, stilted, just plain bad in the same way a

Plus there's the stiltedness of the culture Dostoevsky's characters inhabit. When people are ticked off, for instance, they do
things like "shake their fists" or call each other "scoundrels" or
"fly at" each other.[12] Speakers use exclamation points in quanti-
ties now seen only in comic strips. Social etiquette seems stiff
to the point of absurdity—people are always "calling on" each
other and either "being received" or "not being received" and
obeying rococo conventions of politeness even when they're en-
raged.[13] Everybody's got a long and hard-to-pronounce last
name and Christian name—plus a patronymic, plus sometimes
a diminutive, so you almost have to keep a chart of characters'
names. Obscure military ranks and bureaucratic hierarchies
abound; plus there are rigid and totally weird class distinctions
that are hard to keep straight and understand the implications
of, especially because the economic realities of old Russian society are so strange (as in, e.g., the way even a destitute "former
student" like Raskolnikov or an unemployed bureaucrat like the
Underground Man can somehow afford to have servants).

---

sentence like "'Come on!' she said, addressing her companion and inviting her to
accompany her" is bad?

   If so, why not acknowledge that in English it's still bad and just go ahead and fix
it? Are literary translators not supposed to mess with the original syntax at all? But
Russian is an inflected language—it uses cases and declensions instead of word
order—so translators are already messing with the syntax when they put Dostoevsky's sentences into uninflected English. It's hard to understand why these translations have to be so clunky.

   12. What on earth does it mean to "fly at" somebody? It happens dozens of times
in every FMD novel. What, "fly at" them in order to beat them up? To yell at them?
Why not *say* that, if you're translating?

   13. Q.v. a random example from Pevear and Volokhonsky's acclaimed new Knopf
rendering of *Notes from Underground*:

      "Mr. Ferfichkin, tomorrow you will give me satisfaction for your present
      words!" I said loudly, pompously addressing Ferfichkin.
      "You mean a duel, sir? At your pleasure," the man answered.

The point is that it's not just the death-by-canonization thing: there is real and alienating stuff that stands in the way of our appreciating Dostoevsky and has to be dealt with—either by learning enough about all the unfamiliar stuff that it stops being so confusing, or else by accepting it (the same way we accept racist/sexist elements in some other nineteenth-century books) and just grimacing and reading on anyway.

But the larger point (which, yes, may be kind of obvious) is that some art is worth the extra work of getting past all the impediments to its appreciation; and Dostoevsky's books are definitely worth the work. And this is so not just because of his bestriding the Western canon—if anything, it's despite that. For one thing that canonization and course assignments obscure is that Dostoevsky isn't just great—he's also fun. His novels almost always have ripping good plots, lurid and intricate and thoroughly dramatic. There are murders and attempted murders and police and dysfunctional-family feuding and spies, tough guys and beautiful fallen women and unctuous con men and wasting illnesses and sudden inheritances and silky villains and scheming and whores.

Of course, the fact that Dostoevsky can tell a juicy story isn't enough to make him great. If it were, Judith Krantz and John Grisham would be great fiction writers, and by any but the most commercial standards they're not even very good. The main thing that keeps Krantz and Grisham and lot of other gifted storytellers from being artistically good is that they don't have any talent for (or interest in) characterization—their compelling plots are inhabited by crude and unconvincing stick figures. (In fairness, there are also writers who are good at making complex and fully realized human characters but don't seem able to insert those characters into a believable and interesting plot. Plus others—often among the academic avant-garde—who seem expert/interested

in neither plot nor character, whose books' movement and appeal
depend entirely on rarefied meta-aesthetic agendas.)

The thing about Dostoevsky's characters is that they are *alive*.
By which I don't just mean that they're successfully realized or
developed or "rounded." The best of them live inside us, forever,
once we've met them. Recall the proud and pathetic Raskolnikov,
the naive Devushkin, the beautiful and damned Nastasya of *The
Idiot*,[14] the fawning Lebyedev and spiderish Ippolit of the same
novel; *C&P*'s ingenious maverick detective Porfiry Petrovich
(without whom there would probably be no commercial crime
fiction w/ eccentrically brilliant cops); Marmeladov, the hideous
and pitiful sot; or the vain and noble roulette addict Aleksey Ivanovich of *The Gambler*; the gold-hearted prostitutes Sonya and
Liza; the cynically innocent Aglaia; or the unbelievably repel-
lent Smerdyakov, that living engine of slimy resentment in whom
I personally see parts of myself I can barely stand to look at; or
the idealized and all-too-human Myshkin and Alyosha, the
doomed human Christ and triumphant child-pilgrim, respec-
tively. These and so many other FMD creatures are alive—
retain what Frank calls their "immense vitality"—not because
they're just skillfully drawn types or facets of human beings but
because, acting within plausible and morally compelling plots,
they dramatize the profoundest parts of all humans, the parts
most conflicted, most serious—the ones with the most at stake.

14. (. . . who was, like Faulkner's Caddie, "doomed and knew it," and whose heroism consists in her haughty defiance of a doom she also courts. FMD seems like the
first fiction writer to understand how deeply some people love their own suffering,
how they use it and depend on it. Nietzsche would take Dostoevsky's insight and
make it a cornerstone of his own devastating attack on Christianity, and this is ironic:
in our own culture of "enlightened atheism" we are very much Nietzsche's children,
his ideological heirs, and without Dostoevsky there would have been no Nietzsche,
and yet Dostoevsky is among the most profoundly religious of all writers.)

Plus, without ever ceasing to be 3-D individuals, Dostoevsky's characters manage to embody whole ideologies and philosophies of life: Raskolnikov the rational egoism of the 1860s' intelligentsia, Myshkin mystical Christian love, the Underground Man the influence of European positivism on the Russian character, Ippolit the individual will raging against death's inevitability, Aleksey the perversion of Slavophilic pride in the face of European decadence, and so on and so forth. . . .

The thrust here is that Dostoevsky wrote fiction about the stuff that's really important. He wrote fiction about identity, moral value, death, will, sexual vs. spiritual love, greed, freedom, obsession, reason, faith, suicide. And he did it without ever reducing his characters to mouthpieces or his books to tracts. His concern was always what it is to be a human being—that is, how to be an actual *person,* someone whose life is informed by values and principles, instead of just an especially shrewd kind of self-preserving animal.

** Is it possible really to love other people? If I'm lonely and in pain, everyone outside me is potential relief—I need them. But can you really love what you need so badly? Isn't a big part of love caring more about what the other person needs? How am I supposed to subordinate my own overwhelming need to somebody else's needs that I can't even feel directly? And yet if I can't do this, I'm damned to loneliness, which I definitely don't want . . . so I'm back at trying to overcome my selfishness for self-interested reasons. Is there any way out of this bind? **

It's a well-known irony that Dostoevsky, whose work is famous for its compassion and moral rigor, was in many ways a prick in real life—vain, arrogant, spiteful, selfish. A compulsive gambler, he was usually broke, and whined constantly about his poverty, and was always badgering his friends and colleagues for emergency loans that he seldom repaid, and held petty and long-standing grudges over money, and did things like pawn his delicate wife's winter coat so he could gamble, etc.[15]

But it's just as well known that Dostoevsky's own life was full of incredible suffering and drama and tragedy and heroism. His Moscow childhood was evidently so miserable that in his books Dostoevsky never once sets or even mentions any action in Moscow.[16] His remote and neurasthenic father was murdered by his own serfs when FMD was seventeen. Seven years later, the publication of his first novel,[17] and its endorsement by critics like Belinsky and Herzen, made Dostoevsky a literary star at the same time he was starting to get involved with the Petrashevsky Circle, a group of revolutionary intellectuals who plotted to incite a peasant uprising against the tsar. In 1849, Dostoevsky was

15. Frank doesn't sugar-coat any of this stuff, but from his bio we learn that Dostoevsky's character was really more contradictory than prickish. Insufferably vain about his literary reputation, he was also tormented his whole life by what he saw as his artistic inadequacies; a leech and a spendthrift, he also voluntarily assumed financial responsibility for his stepson, for the nasty and ungrateful family of his deceased brother, and for the debts of *Epoch*, the famous literary journal that he and his brother had co-edited. Frank's new Volume IV makes it clear that it was these honorable debts, rather than general deadbeatism, that sent Mr. and Mrs. FMD into exile in Europe to avoid debtors' prison, and that it was only at the spas of Europe that Dostoevsky's gambling mania went out of control.

16. Sometimes this allergy is awkwardly striking, as in e.g. the start of part 2 of *The Idiot*, when Prince Myshkin (the protagonist) has left St. Petersburg for six full months in Moscow: "of Myshkin's adventures during his absence from Petersburg we can give little information," even though the narrator has access to all sorts of other events outside St. P. Frank doesn't say much about FMD's Muscophobia; it's hard to figure what exactly it's about.

17. = *Poor Folk*, a standard-issue "social novel" that frames a (rather goopy) love story with depictions of urban poverty sufficiently ghastly to elicit the approval of the socialist Left.

arrested as a conspirator, convicted, sentenced to death, and subjected to the famous "mock execution of the Petrashevtsy," in which the conspirators were blindfolded and tied to stakes and taken all the way to the *"Aim!"* stage of the firing-squad process before an imperial messenger galloped in with a supposed "last-minute" reprieve from the merciful tsar. His sentence commuted to imprisonment, the epileptic Dostoevsky ended up spending a decade in balmy Siberia, returning to St. Petersburg in 1859 to find that the Russian literary world had all but forgotten him. Then his wife died, slowly and horribly; then his devoted brother died; then their journal *Epoch* went under; then his epilepsy started getting so bad that he was constantly terrified that he'd die or go insane from the seizures.[18] Hiring a twenty-two-year-old stenographer to help him complete *The Gambler* in time to satisfy a publisher with whom he'd signed an insane deliver-by-a-certain-date-or-forfeit-all-royalties-for-everything-you-ever-wrote contract, Dostoevsky married this lady six months later, just in time to flee *Epoch's* creditors with her, wander unhappily through a Europe whose influence on Russia he despised,[19] have a beloved daughter who

---

18. It is true that FMD's epilepsy—including the mystical illuminations that attended some of his preseizure auras—gets comparatively little discussion in Frank's bio; and reviewers like the *London Times*'s James L. Rice (himself the author of a book on Dostoevsky and epilepsy) have complained that Frank "gives no idea of the malady's chronic impact" on Dostoevsky's religious ideals and their representation in his novels. The question of proportion cuts both ways, though: q.v. the *New York Times Book Review*'s Jan Parker, who spends at least a third of his review of Frank's Volume III making claims like "It seems to me that Dostoevsky's behavior does conform fully to the diagnostic criteria for pathological gambling as set forth in the American Psychiatric Association's diagnostic manual." As much as anything, reviews like these help us appreciate Joseph Frank's own evenhanded breadth and lack of specific axes to grind.

19. Let's not neglect to observe that Frank's Volume IV provides some good personal dirt. W/r/t Dostoevsky's hatred of Europe, for example, we learn that his

died of pneumonia almost right away, writing constantly, penniless, often clinically depressed in the aftermath of tooth-rattling grand mal seizures, going through cycles of manic roulette binges and then crushing self-hatred. Frank's Volume IV relates a lot of Dostoevsky's European tribulations via the journals of his new young wife, Anna Snitkina,[20] whose patience and charity as a spouse might well qualify her as a patron saint of today's codependency groups.[21]

** What is "an American"? Do we have something important in common, as Americans, or is it just that we all happen to live inside the same boundaries and so have to obey the same laws? How exactly is America different from other countries? Is there really something unique about it? What does that uniqueness entail? We talk a lot about our special rights and freedoms, but

---

famous 1867 spat with Turgenev, which was ostensibly about Turgenev's having offended Dostoevsky's passionate nationalism by attacking Russia in print and then moving to Germany, was also fueled by the fact that FMD had previously borrowed fifty thalers from Turgenev and promised to pay him back right away and then never did. Frank is too restrained to make the obvious point: it's much easier to live with stiffing somebody if you can work up a grievance against him.

20. Another bonus: Frank's volumes are replete with marvelous and/or funny tongue-rolling names—Snitkin, Dubolyobov, Strakhov, Golubov, von Voght, Katkov, Nekrasov, Pisarev. One can see why Russian writers like Gogol and FMD made a fine art of epithetic names.

21. Random example from her journal: "'Poor Feodor, he does suffer so much, and is always so irritable, and liable to fly out about trifles. . . . It's of no consequence, because the other days are good, when he is so sweet and gentle. Besides, I can see that when he screams at me it is from illness, not from bad temper.'" Frank quotes and comments on long passages of this kind of stuff, but he shows little awareness that the Dostoevskys' marriage was in certain ways quite sick, at least by 1990s standards—see e.g. "Anna's forbearance, whatever prodigies of self-command it may have cost her, was amply compensated for (at least in her eyes) by Dostoevsky's immense gratitude and growing sense of attachment."

are there also special responsibilities that come with being an American? If so, responsibilities to whom? **

Frank's bio does cover all this personal stuff, in detail, and he doesn't try to downplay or whitewash the icky parts.[22] But his project requires that Frank strive at all times to relate Dostoevsky's personal and psychological life to his books and to the ideologies behind them. The fact that Dostoevsky is first and last an ideological writer[23] makes him an especially congenial subject for Joseph Frank's contextual approach to biography. And the four extant volumes of *Dostoevsky* make it clear that the crucial, catalyzing event in FMD's life, ideologically speaking, was the mock execution of 22 December 1849—a five- or ten-minute interval during which this weak, neurotic, self-involved young writer believed that he was about to die. What resulted inside Dostoevsky was a type of conversion experience, though it gets

---

22. Q.v. also, for instance, Dostoevsky's disastrous passion for the bitch-goddess Appolinaria Suslova, or the mental torsions he performed to justify his casino binges . . . or the fact, amply documented by Frank, that FMD really was an active part of the Petrashevsky Circle and as a matter of fact probably did deserve to be arrested under the laws of the time, this *pace* a lot of other biographers who've tried to claim that Dostoevsky just happened to be dragged by friends to the wrong radical meeting at the wrong time.

23. In case it's not obvious, "ideology" is being used here in its strict, unloaded sense to mean any organized, deeply held system of beliefs and values. Granted, by this sort of definition, Tolstoy and Hugo and Zola and most of the other nineteenth-century titans were also ideological writers. But the big thing about Dostoevsky's gift for character and for rendering the deep conflicts within (not just between) people is that it enables him to dramatize extremely heavy, serious themes without ever being preachy or reductive, i.e., without ever blinking the difficulty of moral/spiritual conflicts or making "goodness" or "redemption" seem simpler than they really are. You need only compare the protagonists' final conversions in Tolstoy's *The Death of Ivan Ilych* and FMD's *Crime and Punishment* in order to appreciate Dostoevsky's ability to be moral without being moralistic.

complicated, because the Christian convictions that inform his writing thereafter are not those of any one church or tradition, and they're also bound up with a kind of mystical Russian nationalism and a political conservatism[24] that led the next century's Soviets to suppress or distort much of Dostoevsky's work.[25]

** Does this guy Jesus Christ's life have something to teach me even if I don't, or can't, believe he was divine? What am I supposed to make of the claim that someone who was God's relative, and so could have turned the cross into a planter or something with just a word, still voluntarily let them nail him up there, and died? Even if we suppose he was divine—did he *know?* Did he know he could have broken the cross with just a word? Did he know in advance that death would just be temporary (because I bet I could climb up there, too, if I knew that an eternity of right-hand bliss lay on the other side of six hours of pain)? But does

24. Here is another subject that Frank treats brilliantly, especially in Vol. III's chapter on *House of the Dead.* Part of the reason FMD abandoned the fashionable socialism of his twenties was his years of imprisonment with the absolute dregs of Russian society. In Siberia, he came to understand that the peasants and urban poor of Russia actually loathed the comfortable upper-class intellectuals who wanted to "liberate" them, and that this loathing was in fact quite justified. (If you want to get some idea of how this Dostoevskyan political irony might translate into modern US culture, try reading *House of the Dead* and Tom Wolfe's "Mau-Mauing the Flak Catchers" at the same time.)

25. The political situation is one reason why Bakhtin's famous *Problems of Dostoevsky's Poetics,* published under Stalin, had to seriously downplay FMD's ideological involvement with his own characters. A lot of Bakhtin's praise for Dostoevsky's "polyphonic" characterizations, and for the "dialogic imagination" that supposedly allowed him to refrain from injecting his own values into his novels, is the natural result of a Soviet critic's trying to discuss an author whose "reactionary" views the State wanted forgotten. Frank, who takes out after Bakhtin at a number of points, doesn't really make clear the constraints that Bakhtin was operating under.

any of that even really matter? Can I still believe in JC or Moham-
med or Whoever even if I don't believe they were actual rela-
tives of God? Except what would that mean: "believe in"? **

What seems most important is that Dostoevsky's near-death experience changed a typically vain and trendy young writer—a
very talented writer, true, but still one whose basic concerns were
for his own literary glory—into a person who believed deeply
in moral/ spiritual values[26] . . . more, into someone who believed
that a life lived without moral/spiritual values was not just incomplete but depraved.[27]

---

26. Not surprisingly, FMD's exact beliefs are idiosyncratic and complicated, and
Joseph Frank is thorough and clear and detailed in explaining their evolution through
the novels' thematics (as in, e.g., the toxic effects of egoistic atheism on the Russian
character in *Notes* and *C &P*; the deformation of Russian passion by worldly Europe
in *The Gambler*; and, in *The Idiot*'s Myshkin and *The Brothers Karamazov*'s Zossima,
the implications of a human Christ subjected literally to nature's physical forces, an
idea central to all the fiction Dostoevsky wrote after seeing Holbein the Younger's
"Dead Christ" at the Basel Museum in 1867).

But what Frank has done really phenomenally well here is to distill the enormous
amounts of archival material generated by and about FMD, making it comprehensive
instead of just using selected bits of it to bolster a particular critical thesis. At one
point, somewhere near the end of Vol. III, Frank even manages to find and gloss
some obscure author-notes for "Socialism and Christianity," an essay Dostoevsky
never finished, that help clarify why he is treated by some critics as a forerunner of
existentialism:

"Christ's incarnation . . . provided a new ideal for mankind, one that has retained
its validity ever since. N.B. Not one atheist who has disputed the divine origin of
Christ has denied the fact that He is the ideal of humanity. The latest on this—
Renan. This is very remarkable." And the law of this new ideal, according to Dostoevsky, consists of "the return to spontaneity, to the masses, but freely. . . . Not forcibly, but on the contrary, in the highest degree willfully and consciously. It is clear that
this higher willfulness is at the same time a higher renunciation of the will."

27. The mature, postconversion Dostoevsky's particular foes were the Nihilists,
the radical progeny of the 1840s' yuppie socialists, whose name (i.e., the Nihilists'

The big thing that makes Dostoevsky invaluable for American readers and writers is that he appears to possess degrees of passion, conviction, and engagement with deep moral issues that we—here, today[28]—cannot or do not permit ourselves. Joseph Frank does an admirable job of tracing out the interplay of factors that made this engagement possible—FMD's own beliefs and talents, the ideological and aesthetic climates of his day, etc. Upon his finishing Frank's books, though, I think that any serious American reader/writer will find himself driven to think hard about what exactly it is that makes many of the novelists of our own place and time look so thematically shallow and lightweight, so morally impoverished, in comparison to Gogol or Dostoevsky (or even to lesser lights like Lermontov and Turgenev). Frank's bio prompts us to ask ourselves why we seem to require of our art an ironic distance from deep convictions or desperate questions, so that contemporary writers have to either make jokes of them or else try to work them in under cover of some formal trick like intertextual quotation or incongruous juxtaposition, sticking the really urgent stuff inside asterisks as part of some multivalent defamiliarization-flourish or some such shit.

Part of the explanation for our own lit's thematic poverty obviously includes our century and situation. The good old

---

name) comes from the same all-negating speech in Turgenev's *Fathers and Sons* that got quoted at the outset. But the real battle was wider, and much deeper. It is no accident that Joseph Frank's big epigraph for Vol. IV is from Kolakowski's classic *Modernity on Endless Trial*, for Dostoevsky's abandonment of utilitarian socialism for an idiosyncratic moral conservatism can be seen in the same basic light as Kant's awakening from "dogmatic slumber" into a radical Pietist deontology nearly a century earlier: "By turning against the popular utilitarianism of the Enlightenment, [Kant] also knew exactly that what was at stake was not any particular moral code, but rather a question of the existence or nonexistence of the distinction between good and evil and, consequently, a question of the fate of mankind."

28. (maybe under our own type of Nihilist spell)

modernists, among their other accomplishments, elevated aesthetics to the level of ethics—maybe even metaphysics—and Serious Novels after Joyce tend to be valued and studied mainly for their formal ingenuity. Such is the modernist legacy that we now presume as a matter of course that "serious" literature will be aesthetically distanced from real lived life. Add to this the requirement of textual self-consciousness imposed by postmodernism[29] and literary theory, and it's probably fair to say that Dostoevsky et al. were free of certain cultural expectations that severely constrain our own novelists' ability to be "serious."

But it's just as fair to observe, with Frank, that Dostoevsky operated under cultural constraints of his own: a repressive government, state censorship, and especially the popularity of post-Enlightenment European thought, much of which went directly against beliefs he held dear and wanted to write about. For me, the really striking, inspiring thing about Dostoevsky isn't just that he was a genius; he was also brave. He never stopped worrying about his literary reputation, but he also never stopped promulgating unfashionable stuff in which he believed. And he did this not by ignoring (now a.k.a. "transcending" or "subverting") the unfriendly cultural circumstances in which he was writing, but by confronting them, engaging them, specifically and by name.

It's actually not true that our literary culture is nihilistic, at least not in the radical sense of Turgenev's Bazarov. For there are certain tendencies we believe are bad, qualities we hate and fear. Among these are sentimentality, naïveté, archaism, fanaticism. It would probably be better to call our own art's culture now one of congenital skepticism. Our intelligentsia[30] distrust strong belief, open conviction. Material passion is one thing, but

29. (whatever exactly that is)
30. (which, given this review's venue, means basically us)

ideological passion disgusts us on some deep level. We believe
that ideology is now the province of the rival SIGs and PACs all
trying to get their slice of the big green pie . . . and, looking
around us, we see that indeed it is so. But Frank's Dostoevsky
would point out (or more like hop up and down and shake his
fist and fly at us and shout) that if this is so, it's at least partly
because we have abandoned the field. That we've abandoned it
to fundamentalists whose pitiless rigidity and eagerness to
judge show that they're clueless about the "Christian values"
they would impose on others. To rightist militias and conspiracy theorists whose paranoia about the government supposes
the government to be just way more organized and efficient than
it really is. And, in academia and the arts, to the increasingly
absurd and dogmatic Political Correctness movement, whose
obsession with the mere forms of utterance and discourse show
too well how effete and aestheticized our best liberal instincts
have become, how removed from what's really important—
motive, feeling, belief.

Have a culminative look at just one snippet from Ippolit's famous "Necessary Explanation" in *The Idiot*:

> "Anyone who attacks individual charity," I began, "attacks
> human nature and casts contempt on personal dignity. But the
> organization of 'public charity' and the problem of individual
> freedom are two distinct questions, and not mutually exclusive.
> Individual kindness will always remain, because it is an indi-
> vidual impulse, the living impulse of one personality to exert a
> direct influence upon another. . . . How can you tell, Bahmu-
> tov, what significance such an association of one personality
> with another may have on the destiny of those associated?"

Can you imagine any of our own major novelists allowing a character to say stuff like this (not, mind you, just as hypocritical

bombast so that some ironic hero can stick a pin in it, but as part of a ten-page monologue by somebody trying to decide whether to commit suicide)? The reason you can't is the reason he wouldn't: such a novelist would be, by our lights, pretentious and overwrought and silly. The straight presentation of such a speech in a Serious Novel today would provoke not outrage or invective, but worse—one raised eyebrow and a very cool smile. Maybe, if the novelist was really major, a dry bit of mockery in *The New Yorker*. The novelist would be (and this is our own age's truest vision of hell) laughed out of town.

So he—we, fiction writers—won't (can't) dare try to use serious art to advance ideologies.[31] The project would be like Menard's *Quixote*. People would either laugh or be embarrassed for us. Given this (and it is a given), who is to blame for the unseriousness of our serious fiction? The culture, the laughers? But they wouldn't (could not) laugh if a piece of morally passionate, passionately moral fiction was also ingenious and radiantly human fiction. But how to make it that? How—for a writer today, even a talented writer today—to get up the guts to even try? There are no formulas or guarantees. There are, however, models. Frank's books make one of them concrete and alive and terribly instructive.

David Foster Wallace
1996

31. We will, of course, without hesitation use art to parody, ridicule, debunk, or criticize ideologies—but this is very different.

ACKNOWLEDGMENTS

We would like to thank Slavic Languages and Literatures Department at Stanford University; Anne Savarese, Ellen Foos, and the entire editorial team at Princeton University Press; Frank Gruber; Robin F. Miller for her insightful foreword; and Bonnie Nadell (of Hill Nadell Literary Agency) for the permission to include David Foster Wallace's essay.

INDEX

of, 30; humiliation in, 23, 38, 39; inner conflict in, 35, 41–42, 44; and *Notes from Underground*, 96, 97; psychology in, 33, 40–42, 54; revised version of, 29; semicomic chapter headings in, 29–30; society in, 30, 33, 34, 35, 38, 40, 43, 73; subtitle of, 30
doubles, 32, 33, 41, 120, 167–68, 176
dramatic monologue, 84

Edel, Leon, *Henry James*, vii
educated people, xiii, 2, 3–4, 15, 80–81, 105
education, Western, 4, 5–6, 58, 63, 80–81
ego/egoism, 35; annihilation of, 134; and atheism, 205n26; in *The Brothers Karamazov*, 160, 161, 165, 166, 176; in *Crime and Punishment*, 109, 119, 122, 127; and faith, 164; and family, 136, 140; in *The Idiot*, 127, 136, 137, 142, 143, 144, 149, 150, 151; of intelligentsia, 199; and love, 137, 138, 140–41; and *Notes from Underground*, 74, 78, 95, 96, 97, 98; of radicals, 115; rational, 79, 106; and reason, 161; and sexuality, 140–41; of suffering, 143, 144, 151; transcendence of, 164; and Turgenev, 106
Eliot, George, 49
Ellmann, Richard, *James Joyce*, vii, 189–90
emotions, 48; in *The Brothers Karamazov*, 162, 166, 175; and Chernyshevsky, 79; and *Crime and Punishment*, 109, 116, 117, 123, 124; and *The House of the Dead*, 65, 69; and *The Idiot*, 127; importance of, 66; and *Notes from Underground*, 85, 88, 92, 97, 113; and *Poor Folk*, 22, 26; and religion, 68, 175
English novel, 102

envy, 89, 90
epilepsy, 55, 126, 142, 145–46, 148, 152
epistolary form, 14–15
Epokha (Epoch), 84, 98, 110, 200n15, 201
eschatology, 54, 55, 56, 66, 141, 142, 158
Europe, 80–81, 85, 156, 201, 202
European culture, xiii, 2, 3, 42, 151, 199, 207. *See also* West/Western culture
European literature, 8–9, 96
evil, 63, 113, 149, 155, 170, 178, 180
existentialism, xi, 188
Expressionism, xi

faith, 199; and egoism, 164; and Euclidian understanding, 164; in *The Idiot*, 146, 148, 149; and Kierkegaard, 173; leap of, 160, 161, 166; and love, 164; and morality, 148; necessity of, 160; and reason, 148, 149, 159, 172–73. See also *The Brothers Karamazov* (Dostoevsky); conscience; religion
family: accidental, 155; in *The Brothers Karamazov*, 155, 161–62, 172; and *Crime and Punishment*, 104, 117; and egoism, 136, 140; in *The Idiot*, 137; and morality, 155; and *A Raw Youth*, 155
fantastic, 32, 33
fantastic realism, 28–29
fantasy, 35, 96
fathers, 161–62
fathers and sons, 154–57, 172
Faulkner, William, 198n14
Faust, xi. *See also* Goethe, Johann Wolfgang von, *Faust*
Fedotov, G. P., *The Russian Religious Mind*, 131
Feuerbach, Ludwig, 7, 78; *The Essence of Christianity*, 49–50
Flaubert, Gustave, ix

Petrashevsky Circle, 7–8, 45–46, 47–48, 51, 200, 203n22
phalanstery, 46
philosophy, 1, 112, 156, 188. *See also* metaphysics
physiological sketches, 12, 16, 20, 21
picaresque, 154
Pisarev, Dmitry, 105–6, 107, 108, 109, 111, 113, 126
Pisemsky, Aleksey, 84
pity, 2; in *The Brothers Karamazov*, 167, 178, 181; in *Crime and Punishment*, 117, 118; in *The Idiot*, 128, 137, 139, 150; in *Poor Folk*, 26, 34; and *Underground Man*, 97. *See also* compassion
Plato, 137–38
Poe, Edgar Allan, 33; "William Wilson," 32
Polish uprising (1863), 107
politics, x, xiii, xxii, 59, 90, 126, 204. *See also* Petrashevsky Circle; social-political issues
Poor Folk (Dostoevsky), 5, 11, 14–27, 28, 198, 200n17; compassion in, 10, 21, 61; and *Crime and Punishment*, 103; and *The Double*, 33–34, 36, 43; God in, 21, 27, 53; Gogol and, 9, 12, 14, 17, 18, 20, 21, 23, 25, 26, 30, 31; and *The Idiot*, 149; justice in, 21, 26, 43; morality in, 17, 18, 19, 24, 42, 46; and *Notes from Underground*, 72, 94; pity in, 26, 34; society in, 17, 21, 24, 26–27, 34, 72, 73
poor people, 204n24; and *Crime and Punishment*, 104; and *The Double*, 38, 43; and Pisarev, 106; in *Poor Folk*, 14, 16–17, 22–23, 25, 34, 54. *See also* lower classes
populism, 156, 159, 163

positivism, 165, 199
postmodernism, 207
prostitutes/prostitution: and Chernyshevsky, 95; and *Crime and Punishment*, 99, 110, 120, 121, 124; and *Notes from Underground*, 74, 75, 94, 95, 98, 120; in *Winter Notes on Summer Impressions*, 82
Proust, Marcel, ix
psychology, x; in *Crime and Punishment*, 64, 111, 112, 113; in *The Double*, 33, 40–42, 54; dramatization of, 72; and FD's mock execution, 126; and *The House of the Dead*, 69; and ideology, 44, 81; and *The Idiot*, 126; and *Notes from Underground*, 73, 85, 90, 94; in *Poor Folk*, 26; and *A Raw Youth*, 156; and Russian history, 82; social causes of, 85; and *Winter Notes on Summer Impressions*, 81
Pushkin, Alexander Sergeyevich, xv, 9, 10, 95; and Gogol, 31; and *The Idiot*, 131; and Pisarev, 106; and *Poor Folk*, 11, 19, 26; "Poor Knight," 132n10; *The Queen of Spades*, 108–9; self-sacrifice in, 16, 17, 43; social pathos of, 13; "The Stationmaster," 11–12, 26; suffering in, 16, 20, 23

Radcliffe, Ann, 102
radical intelligentsia, xii, 76, 126; and *The Brothers Karamazov*, 170; and *Crime and Punishment*, 100; and European ideas, 85; and laws of nature, 134; and *Notes from Underground*, 188; and Polish uprising, 107; and Turgenev, 106; and Western ideas, 109. *See also* intelligentsia

social-political issues, 77, 79; and class division, 61; and *Crime and Punishment*, 111; and *The Idiot*, 126; and morality, 76; and *Notes from Underground*, 90. *See also* politics

social-psychological issues: and *Notes from Underground*, 85; in *Poor Folk*, 26–27, 72

society, x, xii, 2, 188; in *The Brothers Karamazov*, 150, 155, 158; and characters, 29; and class division, 60–61; communal organization of, 47; and *Crime and Punishment*, 101, 103, 109, 110, 111, 112, 113; and *The Double*, 30, 33, 34, 35, 38, 40, 43, 73; and eschatology, 55; in FD's early vs. later works, 53; and Feuerbach, 49–50; in Gogol, 32; hierarchy of, 73; and *The House of the Dead*, 59, 63; and *The Idiot*, 126, 130, 137, 148; and *Notes from Underground*, 84–85, 90, 95, 96; and novel, 9; and personal morality, 56–57; and Petrashevsky Circle, 46; and Pisarev, 106, 107; in *Poor Folk*, 17, 21, 24, 26–27, 34, 72, 73; of Pushkin, 13; and *A Raw Youth*, 156; and religion, 53; revolt against, 103; in *roman-feuilleton*, 102; socialist reconstruction of, 47; in *Winter Notes on Summer Impressions*, 81, 82, 83

Soviet Union, 83

Spanish Inquisition, 159

Speshnev, Nikolay, 52

spirituality, 29, 190, 199, 203n23, 205; in *The Brothers Karamazov*, 160, 174, 175, 179; and Chernyshevsky, 83; crisis of, 134; in *The Idiot*, 151; and *Poor Folk*, 24; in Russian culture, 3; and state, 175; in *Winter Notes on*

Summer Impressions, 82. *See also* religion

Stendhal (Marie-Henri Beyle), 104

Stoicism, 56

St. Petersburg, 6, 16, 17, 26, 30, 37, 102, 200n16, 201; Peter and Paul Fortress, 8n6, 51, 54n4

stream-of-consciousness, 43, 68

suffering: in *The Brothers Karamazov*, 158, 165, 176, 178, 180; of Christ, 56, 131, 140; and *Crime and Punishment*, 116, 117, 121, 122; and *The Double*, 43; egoism of, 143, 144, 151; and *The House of the Dead*, 67; in Hugo, 130; in *The Idiot*, 126, 141, 143, 144, 150, 151; and interim ethics, 121; and *Notes from Underground*, 97; in *Poor Folk*, 16, 20, 23

suicide, 68, 124, 143, 144, 155, 199

supernatural, 13, 32, 168–69, 173–74, 181

Surrealism, xi

Suslova, Appolinaria, 203n22

Tolstoy, Leo, xv, 2, 4, 69, 114; *The Death of Ivan Ilych*, 203n23; *War and Peace*, 4, 170

tragedy, 1, 53, 54, 97

tsar, xii, 10, 77, 79, 200

Turgenev, Ivan, xv, 112–13, 114, 201n19; *Fathers and Sons*, 106–7, 108, 111, 126, 187, 205–6n27, 207

United States, 47, 90–91

upper class, 204n24; and *Crime and Punishment*, 124; and *The Double*, 37; and epistolary form, 14–15; in Gogol, 13; and *The House of the Dead*, 58–61; as overcoming class differences, 60–61; peasants' hatred of, 58, 59–61, 76; in *Poor Folk*, 22–23;